Enc

Since 1988 Pastc instrumental in my life. As a career missionary, virgil has encouraged, supported and prayed for my family. He has been a mentor and a confidant. His depth of faith and wisdom in Christ has been a resource as we have discussed the challenges and complexities of mission work today. Pastor Virgil's understanding of personal relationships and how to redeem them through the love of Christ and prayer has spoken volumes to me. Pastor Virgil has had a global impact through more than 100 missionaries. The small town of Shell Lake, Wisconsin is on the map of international missions because of his vision and hard work. I am honored to count Pastor Virgil as one of my closest friends. He is a man of God who has faithfully served the church and his community for 50 years. May his biography bless you as you read Called to be Faithful which reveals the motivation of his heart.

Steve Salowitz
Field Operations Director of Seed Company for Africa and the Americas

So many of us are struggling to fulfill the plan of God in their lives without realizing their God-given call. With many personal enriched experiences, Pastor Virgil Amundson has challenged the readers to be faithful to their callings as "Faithfulness brings Fruitfulness."

Bishop Julius Morar
President, Peace Missions International, Inc.

The year was 1973, and I traveled to Wisconsin to be part of a youth camp. Little did I know that I would meet Pastor Virgil Amundson and would become lifelong friends. Through the years we have shared pulpits, attended conferences, hunted and fished together. Brother Virgil has been a mentor to me and has invested words of wisdom into my life that have helped shape me into the man I have become.

Brother Virgil is truly a "man's man." He is never at a loss for words. He has always been there for my family and has been a faithful friend. My wife Marilyn and my four sons always look forward to spending time with him.

Behind every great man, there is a great woman! Linda Amundson is a wonderful wife who has supported her husband through the ups and downs of life. She has been blessed by the Lord to know how to speak into Virgil's life to help him excel in the ministry. All of their children and grandchildren are serving the Lord. What a great testimony!

Richard W. Beatty
Founding Pastor, Abundant Life Church

I have had the privilege of knowing Pastor Virgil Amundson for over 58 years. We have ministered together, hunted together, fished together, laughed together and cried together. We have fathered two children who are now husband and wife and from whom we share three beautiful grandchildren. There is probably no other fellow pastor that I know any better than Virgil. As he has been writing this account of his life, I have watched him become more aware of how, because he yielded his life to Jesus Christ, his life has been a very pivotal part in the spiritual lives of so many people. As he has seen this, he understood to an even greater degree how God can use us as we yield our lives to Him more and more each day. As you read his story, understand it is not what he has done, but his life is truly an example of what God has done through a yielded life. His obedience to God has made him an instrument whom God has used through all these years in a powerful way that has impacted the lives of so many. My wife, Lois, and I are blessed beyond words to be a part of Pastor Virgil and Linda's lives. We love and appreciate the both of them so much. Remember, as you read this account of his life, see what God can do with someone who yields his life wholly to Him. We serve the same God.

Dr. Arvid Moin
Communion With God Leaders Network

CALLED

──── TO BE ────

FAITHFUL

50 years of pastoring a small town church that has touched the world

PASTOR VIRGIL AMUNDSON

Published by Virgil Amundson: *N3367 Deer Path Rd., Sarona, WI 54840 • virgilamundson2@gmail.com*

Graphics & book production: *David Bergsland, Bergsland Design http://www.bergsland.org*

Copyediting: *Steve Mathisen, OddSock Proofreading and Copyediting http://oddsock.me*

Bible translations used in *Called to be Faithful*:

New King James Version (NKJV)

King James Version (KJV)

Revised Standard Version (RSV)

New Living Translation (NLT)

New American Standard Bible (NASB)

Cover Photo

The photo on the book cover was taken on Alder Lake in the Boundary Waters Canoe Wilderness Area in northern Minnesota.

My missionary friend, Steve Salowitz, had asked me to be part of a camping and canoeing expedition with four members of the Field Operations Leadership team of the Seed Company, a division of Wycliffe Bible Translators. Their purpose was to discuss a mission's strategy for Bible Translation across the globe. My assignment was to be the fishing guide and to share some of my pastoral experiences around the campfire during the evenings.

The picture was taken as the early morning sun was peeking through the fog and reflecting off the lake. I'm standing on the rocks off the island where our camp was set up.

It was a serene moment to reflect upon God's faithfulness and His goodness to allow me to experience His awesome creation.

Dedication

I want to dedicate my first book in honor of the most important person in my life.

My wife Linda has stood beside me from the first day that we began our ministry in Barronett, Wisconsin in 1966. The town was less than sixty people. The church building was made of red brick from the old Barronett brickyard and was constructed in the mid-1930's. The church was not insulated and had men's and lady's outdoor toilets. This made it difficult for Linda and our two small children to meet their bathroom needs during the cold winter months. The small congregation was mostly older people.

Linda has always been supportive and loyal to help me carry out what I believed God had called me to do. She was never negative or even tried to discourage me from going on and giving my best to build up a work that had very little potential for growth.

Linda has been my greatest encourager and manager to my life all through our years in ministry. Her time and attention to the children growing up has paid off with rich rewards in their lives of faith, sound character, and entrepreneurship. I am forever grateful for the wonderful wife God has blessed me with.

You never stopped reminding me to write and publish the book about our life and ministry of fifty years. Thank you for all of your encouragement.

Contents

Acknowledgments

I needed lots of help to move forward with plans to write my first book. A lot of encouragement and direction came from Evangelist Tom Shanklin. I'm grateful to Tom for his assistance in helping me with recommendations of an editor and book designer. Thanks Tom for your relentless encouragement to get it finished.

Thank you to my granddaughter, Adelle Hodgett, for translating my scribbled hand-written copies and typing every chapter. You are so easy to work with. You really helped your Papa.

Thanks to Adelle's husband, Josiah Hodgett, for taking the time to proofread everything and help make the necessary corrections.

Special thanks to my wife, Linda, for reading through all the rough drafts and keeping me on target with the correct facts. You are such a big part of the story and my life inspiration and love at all times! You gently pushed me to complete each chapter and complimented me on each one. We share this story together.

Foreword

Called to be Faithful highlights the ministry of Rev. Virgil and Linda Amundson in story form so it's palatable to every reader. Their ministry is based in a small community in northern Wisconsin called Shell Lake. From this rural town in the north woods a mission has been launched that reaches across the country and around the world. Narratives of touching people locally and abroad with the full gospel are what this book is all about.

Having had the privilege of Virgil Amundson as my personal mentor and my family pastor for over three decades is a blessing indeed. My wife Sandy and I were commissioned out from the Shell Lake Full Gospel Church to establish a Full Gospel New Testament Church called Northern Lights Christian Center in Hayward, WI. Pastor Amundson has walked beside me, been an encouragement to me, as well as served as an overseer in the various ministries of our local assembly.

Called to be Faithful is a book that compiles a lifetime of motivational biographies and faith-filled stories that will be talked about for a long time. It shows us how real people from rural USA can bring the gospel to our communities with faith in God. It also shows us how we can make a difference in the nations of the world by reaching them from right here at home.

I certainly do recommend reading this book Called to be Faithful. Its stories and personal experiences will inspire your heart to serve God wholeheartedly.

Timothy L. Warner, Th.B., M.C.ED., Ph.D.
Pastor, Northern Lights Christian Center, Hayward, WI
Chairman, International Ministerial Association

Preface

Friends and family have encouraged me to write the story of my life while serving as pastor of Shell Lake Full Gospel Church for 50 years.

So many wonderful adventures and stories of faith, challenges, and miracles truly should be worth writing about. The stories in Called to be Faithful are written to inspire the reader to believe for what little we have to offer into God's hands will become greatly multiplied with what He can accomplish with it.

It's an amazing story of love, compassion, and willing people who opened their hearts to get involved in something that is bigger than themselves. It's a story about world adventures that come from God-given opportunities to make a difference in people's lives around the world.

Called to be Faithful is a story about the blessings and rewards that come from obeying God's call and not giving up when progress seems to come to an end.

The story is an autobiography about my life experiences that contain both the heartaches and joys of fifty years as pastor of one church. I'm delighted to share them with you.

Pastor Virgil Amundson
Shell Lake, Wisconsin
September 2016

Chapter 1
Embrace Your Seasons

This begins the story of the seasons of ministry that I have experienced as the founding pastor of Shell Lake Full Gospel Church. It has been fifty years of serving in a small community of fewer than twelve hundred people, living life in a fishbowl, where it seems that everyone knows everything about you and is aware of everything you do.

This is a story of life experiences that contain heartache, tremendous challenges, and grand victories as God has moved through the seasons of my life and the seasons of change for a small town congregation that has touched the world with the gospel of Christ.

Everyone will experience different seasons throughout their life. Nothing will ever stay the same. God intended it to be that way. Scripture tells us, "To everything there is a season, a time for every purpose under heaven" (Ecclesiastes 3:1 NKJV).

In the natural, God created every season for its own purpose. When that season is finished, a new season comes. There are seasons of preparing, and to plant; a season of cultivating, and a season of harvest.

In Wisconsin, we have four completely different, yet beautiful seasons. They are the summer, autumn, winter, and spring seasons. Each has their separate time and their own beauty.

The scripture says, "While the earth remains, seedtime and harvest, cold and heat, winter and summer, and day and night shall not cease" (Genesis 8:22 RSV).

Seasons often repeat themselves. They will most likely come around again. That means we will have another opportunity to grow and do better in the way we handle things through what we learned in that previous season.

I don't consider myself to be a wise man, but I certainly have gained some wisdom in the way I handle the life that I've been handed and the ministry God has given me to help others.

Seasons in my life are similar to four cycles of church life that we as a church body have experienced over the past fifty years.—Let me call them the cycles of preparation, gathering, sifting, and maturity.

The Preparation season is where either myself and/or the church experiences a time where it seems that nothing is happening. It is a time when there is no growth, no success, with much hard labor, but no apparent results. It can be a discouraging time when it brings us to our knees to admit to God that we are powerless and hopelessly dependent upon Him to change our condition (I have been at that place a few times).

The Gathering season is the time where, without any explanation, the church seems to grow rapidly, and people become excited over God's favor and blessing. A time when we are unable to assess what we did to make such success and increase happen. We spend our time searching for ways to make changes necessary to accommodate the increase taking place. It's a time of renewal and outpouring of God's grace and the Holy Spirit, and people are full of love and compassion toward all the new people who gather into the church.

The Sifting cycle is the season when people for lack of clear reason, begin to shift and move on. Some will move to other churches. Some will decide that church isn't for them anymore. Whatever the reason, there are those who are loved in the church, but who decide or feel directed to other ministries. It's a painful time for pastors who are unable to stop the moving or shifting no matter how much prayer they offer or counsel they give. It can leave pastors feeling like failures, and we have to guard against self-blame, rejection, and discouragement. It's an uncertain time.

The Maturity cycle takes place after the sifting process, and this could be considered the best season of all. This is the time when people who have been idle observers become activated with their gifts and service to help in all aspects of church life. New ministries and elders and servant leaders emerge to a new level of involvement. The church becomes strong in faith with healthy attitudes that promote unity and blessings upon families and upon leadership.

Each of these cycles has taken place at least three times during our ministry. I have learned that cycles and seasons are inevitable in everyone's life. But it is only a season. A new season is going to come. I have had to learn not to fight against the seasons that have been hard and painful, but to embrace those seasons until God changes it. I believe that God wants us to honor the season we are in. Our future harvest and blessings are dependent upon our faithfulness in the season we are in.

The scripture says, "Enjoy prosperity while you can, but when hard times strike, realize that both come from God. Remember that nothing is certain in life" (Ecclesiastes 7:14 NLT).

Through the years I have attempted to embrace every season by believing that God had a greater purpose for my life. In every season I have tried to make the most of every opportunity. That is how you maximize your season.

It was in my first season of preparation as our work in Shell Lake began that God was teaching me both patience and trust in the midst of some early discouragement. It was during that testing season when I didn't know anything about getting a new church started that God gave me a personal affirmation from Job 8:7. "Though thy beginning was small, yet thy latter end should greatly increase" (KJV). I have kept that word in my heart as a personal promise from God.

The season of my "latter end" of the pastoral ministry at Shell Lake Full Gospel Church is now upon me. It culminates our fiftieth year since my wife Linda and I and our two babies, Teresa and Brent began driving from Rice Lake to Barronett, Wisconsin to pastor a small flock of people who were part of a church called Apostolic Faith Tabernacle.

Our journey began in July of 1966. Our season of ministry began in a small uninsulated brick building with a coal furnace in the basement and a two-hole outdoor unheated privy for our inconvenience. The population of the Barronett community was fifty people.

We made the trek from Rice Lake to Barronett three times weekly for two and a half years to hold services. It was a drive of twenty-five minutes each way. We closed down the church in Barronett in August 1969 and moved my family and seven of the church members to Shell Lake.

Linnea Rydberg, Louis Schoenhals, and I signed a six-thousand-dollar loan to purchase the historic St John's Lutheran Church and parsonage for the sum of eleven thousand dollars. The parsonage would be our home for the next nine years. Our daughter and third child, Angel, was born in 1970. Another season in our lives had begun.

Chapter 2
Year of Transition

It was early in December of 1968 that I was driving down Highway 63 somewhere between Shell Lake and Barronett when I suddenly was overwhelmed by God's presence which caused me to start weeping uncontrollably. I could not drive because of the tears, so I pulled the van I was driving to the side of the road and continued to weep for a few minutes.

The overwhelming presence of God flooded into my heart, and I asked the Lord, "What do you want me to do?" I remember getting back onto the highway and in just a short time I heard words speak very clearly into my spirit that said to me, "Son, 1969 will be a transitional year!"

I didn't know what to do with that. My family was living in Rice Lake, and I had been driving back and forth to Barronett to minister for nearly two years. I was working in sales and delivery for a small notions distributor in Rice Lake known as Brown Sales. I had been with them for nine years while also doing studies and training for the ministry.

I had under a wonderful pastor who spent much time preparing me and mentoring me for God's calling in my life. His name was Pastor Caleb Warner who was married to my father's sister. Her name was Florence. Pastor Warner died in 1980 and my father continued to look after his sister until both of them passed away in 2014. They were both in their mid-nineties. My mother also passed away in 2014. Both my mother and father were a godly influence in my life, especially with their prayers and solid integrity. My dad served as an elder in his church faithfully for sixty-eight years until his health began to fail. My mother was a woman of great faith in the promises of God's word.

I had been a frail, asthmatic child until I reached twelve years of age. I remember many nights when I would not sleep because of choking and breathing difficulty. Mother would stay up with me through the night to hold my shoulders back so I could get air and she would pray over me that Jesus would heal me from asthma. I would feel better in the morning, and I just believed that it was mother's prayers that had helped me. The big breakthrough came for me when I was twelve years old. We were on a church picnic at Narrows Park in Rice Lake. I was playing a softball game with some young people when I suddenly felt weak and slumped down against a tree. An attack of asthma had hit me, and my mother saw me slumped against the tree. She ran over to me, and I remember her yelling the name of Jesus and saying something against the devil; she made a loud command for my body to receive healing. In minutes I was playing ball again with normal breathing. My story is from that day to this day, over sixty years ago, I have never had any more problems with asthma. I was healed! God had put great faith in my heart to believe Him for miracles throughout the years of our ministry.

I wondered why I had heard the voice say, "1969 would be a year of transition." Was God preparing me for a big change in my life? I had no idea as to what it would be. I'm reminded of the scripture in which God says, ""For My thoughts are not your thoughts, Nor are your ways My ways …" (Isaiah 55:8 NKJV).

I resigned my thoughts to just letting God do whatever He had in His plans to bringing the change that He had in mind for us.

While serving the church in Barronett, I had an opportunity to start radio broadcasts every Sunday morning on the new Shell Lake radio station. The broadcasts were called "Christ is the Answer." I continued to do them for the next thirty years.

In those days the taped broadcasts were made on reel to reel tapes. When we lived in Rice Lake, I would make the tapes in our home and drive to Shell Lake on Saturdays to deliver it to the station to be aired on Sunday.

One Saturday night in April 1969 we took the tape to Shell Lake where the station owner, Chuck Lutz, was waiting for us. That evening Sheldon Dwyer and Pastor C.L. Warner rode to Shell Lake with me. We dropped the tape off and, out of the clear blue, Pastor Warner asked

Chuck Lutz if he knew of any church buildings that might be for sale in Shell Lake. I was amused by his question while thinking, "What chance could there be for that to happen?" To my surprise, Mr. Lutz had heard about a church in town that might be merging with a church in Spooner. He did not know if the church was for sale. He did give us the name of a church board member and we called him immediately to inquire about it. The man, whose name was Ernest Norton, informed us that the church would possibly be put up for sale.

In the succeeding months, we were able to negotiate the sale of the old St. John's Lutheran church and parsonage next door for the sum of eleven thousand dollars for both buildings.

In August of 1969, my family and I left the city where we had lived all of our lives and moved to little Shell Lake. We opened up the doors of our first service in what would become known as Shell Lake Full Gospel Church. The church was named "Full Gospel," because of a successful international parachurch ministry known as the "Full Gospel Businessmen's Association." The church is independent from any denominational organization.

The church was set up to be an autonomous, independent, self-governing body, with oversight by the pastor and elders. This system has successfully stood in place throughout the church's existence.

God's word concerning "Transition" in 1969 had come to pass for my family and me as we settled into the Shell Lake community to begin a new destiny in our lives.

We could never have perceived what God had planned for the future, from the humblest beginnings of Full Gospel Church to its international impact and influence with mission works around the world.

The Old Church Building

The old brick church building in Barronett was sold for four hundred dollars and later excavated, leaving only a small lot left with pine trees as a remnant to where our ministry was started.

God's word would be confirmed concerning our small beginnings. He has increased our latter days and has exceeded any expectations we have had. He truly is "... able to do exceedingly abundantly above all that we ask or think according to His power that works in us" (Ephesians 3:20 KJV).

Chapter 3
Preparing the Man

I feel like my whole life has been in training for becoming the man God wants me to be. God uses people in our lives to shape us through instruction, correction, discipline, and encouragement.

I once heard Evangelist Lowell Lundstrom say that "God is more interested in making the man than He is in making his ministry." Our character is more important than our charisma. Through the years I have seen the tragedy of honored and trusted charismatic leaders fail morally or financially. It always shakes people's faith and causes unbelievers to lose confidence in Christian leaders when they fail. When a righteous man falls, he may rise again but most often his work and ministry never rises to the level that they previously had before their fall. The most important part of a leader's legacy is their own family. We impart to them what we are, more than what we do. Our teaching comes from our knowledge, but our influence comes out of our lives. Integrity, honesty, and loyalty are among the best qualities of a leader.

My pastor was a spiritual father and mentor to me in the early years of ministry. He warned me of the three major pitfalls to a ministry. He called them the three "W's"—Wine, Women, and Wealth. The dangers of alcohol, lust, and love of money or greed can take a leader down unless safeguards for protection from the pitfalls have been set.

My pastor challenged me to study God's word and to take intentional time for fasting and prayer. He knew that when a person disciplines himself in these areas, it helps to set up greater disciplines and benefits them morally, mentally, and spiritually in their personal lives.

He also knew how to burst my pride when I was a novice in the ministry. When he gave me opportunities to preach, I would always speak with a lot of zeal and excitement. Once I preached about Jonah and all through the message I kept referring to Jonah as being in the "whale of a belly." People were chuckling, and I thought that I was making a hit with my message. I had preached it with a lot of zeal. I didn't know about my mistake until pastor notified me. I was not prepared for his criticism of my message. I asked him how he thought it went. He said to me, "Son, you were like a ten-ton truck delivering an empty load." I could not pull anything over my pastor. I learned to put more time in studying for my sermons.

My pastor showed his confidence in me. Louis Schoenhals from Cumberland came to my pastor and asked him if he would release me from my youth leadership in the church to come and pastor the congregation in Barronett. I know it was a sacrifice for my pastor to release me from the youth ministry. It turned out that I would never return back to the Rice Lake church after leaving to become pastor of the Barronett church in 1966.

My wife, Linda, is an intuitive and very loyal woman. She is not the out-front type person like I am. She has always felt that her role was to support my ministry from behind the scenes and to fill the needs of our children, especially in areas where I was negligent. I think that I was often negligent because I would often put ministry and self-interests ahead of my family. This put our marriage in crisis in the early years because of lack of attentiveness toward my family's needs. We were never unfaithful to each other. We have always enjoyed our physical relationship through the years. I just didn't sacrifice enough of my busyness to give the proper amount of time and attention to them.

Looking back at how fast our children grew up and left the home, one of my few regrets is that I didn't spend more personal and individual time with them. I owe it to God's grace and a loving and attentive wife that our children all love and serve the Lord. They all have good marriages of their own and have produced for us eight grandchildren and two great-grandchildren thus far.

The scriptures teach us that church leaders "must manage his own family well, having children who respect and obey them. If a man cannot manage his own household, how can he take care of God's church?" (1 Timothy 3:4-5 NLT)

The leaders that are most deeply respected are the ones who have solid marriages and who invest time and respect into their children's lives. This has been an important concern in developing and mentoring leaders for ministry. I think we have been successful in building strong leaders with solid marriages and respected families. It is ineffective to export a gospel that does not work for us in our own families. This is why Evangelist Lowell Lundstrom said that "God is more interested in preparing the man before he prepares his ministry."

I have been privileged to establish accountability relationships with many godly men in ministry. Pastor Paul Tucker is one of my longtime friends, teacher, and mentor. Paul has an anointed prophetic ministry and is a leader to hundreds of ministries from around the world. Paul dedicated our first church in Shell Lake in 1969. We still communicate regularly and have traveled together occasionally to minister in other countries. I feel obligated to Paul Tucker to remain a minister of integrity and purity that honors God and exemplifies the good in ministry.

Dr. Arvid Moin is another accountability friend. Arvid came to Shell Lake in 1982 and joined the ministerial staff. His wife, Lois, and their three children settled here for ten years. Arvid's background as a pastor of several Methodist churches helped me to handle some situations that his expertise was able to resolve. God gave us a unity of spirit and love for each other that allowed us to be open and transparent with each other. We both felt an unspoken accountability but would warn each other of any potential danger that might trip one of us up. We were committed to not betray the trust we had for each other.

Arvid possessed an excellent teaching gift, and we both realized a vision fulfilled when we were able to start a Bible training school. It was called Indianhead School of the Bible. It continued for several years. His expertise was teaching on "Hearing God's Voice."

In 1992 the Moins moved to Rice Lake to become the pastor of New Life Church there. The previous leadership had had a moral failure, and the church was embroiled in litigation. Arvid poured himself into saving the church from its quagmire. He continued serving there until turning the church over to Pastor Bob Pitman. The church is now a thriving and vibrant congregation in that city. The Moin's son, Steven, was married to our daughter, Angel, in 1993 and they live in Blaine, Minnesota.

Another group of men and women I am connected with in ministry are members of the International Ministerial Association (I.M.A.) I was ordained and licensed in ministry with the I.M.A. in April 1967.

I pursued more than just a membership in this ministry association by becoming active with some of its functions. I first served on the district board and became a district chairperson for a few years. We occasionally invited some of the member ministers to minister in Shell Lake. Our church has built some good relationships with many I.M.A. ministers. I have also had many opportunities to minister in some I.M.A. churches through the years.

I was elected to the general board of the I.M.A. at age forty-three and have served on and off the general board. I will terminate my service to the general board in 2017, after serving for thirty years.

The I.M.A. has been an important connection for building quality relationships with pastors and church leaders who have become lifetime friends. Most of our connections have taken place at district conferences and retreats. The annual general conferences are held each year in different places around the United States. I have been honored to speak at several of those conferences.

Some of the great men of God who were leaders in the I.M.A. are now gone. These men were spiritual giants in my eyes. Allow me to honor such men as Richard Reneau, James Holt, Worthy and David Rowe, Glen Yeazel, A.D. VanHoose, Art Smith, and Paul Winter. These dear men trusted me as a spiritual son and cast their influence of solid, godly character into my life. They gave me opportunities to provide ideas and input into the direction for the future of the I.M.A. I will always be grateful for the years I have been associated with the brethren in the I.M.A.

Chapter 4
Living Life and Loving It

No one has ever accused me of being a stereo-typical pastor. I'm not sure what that looks like, but I'm pretty sure that I'm not one of them. I have always been a high-energy, active person who loves life and enjoys many forms of recreation. I grew up in sports. Basketball and baseball were among my favorite sports. Swimming was my summer passion growing up.

My father taught me to hunt and fish, so that has become my adult avocation, apart from the ministry. I enjoy most all sports, including golf. Did I mention golf? I'm not saying that I am good at any of these sports, but they have certainly served as a diversion and relief from the rigors and tensions of the ministry. I'm a person who enjoys having someone else with me to enjoy life's simple pleasures. This has provided many opportunities to spend time away from the church with guys from all walks of life. Believers and unbelievers alike.

Cross-pollination is something very important to me. Jesus spent the majority of his time with his disciples but also cross-pollinated with the publicans and sinners by giving them some of his time. I have often used my leisure time to join with friends who are not of my spiritual persuasion. Whether it is inviting them to join me on a fishing outing to Canada, a hunting trip out west, or just a golf outing, I always enjoy having a blend of guys who know the Lord along with some guys who may not know the Lord. I have seen many men over the years who have gained confidence enough with me to admit their needs and accept my offer to pray for them. I love those opportunities.

I've known some ministers and pastors whose whole life becomes consumed by the ministry. They have few outlets, no hobbies, and no place to release tension. Did I say that the ministry has tensions? Okay then, how about stress? The fact is that the ministry is one of the top vocations for stress. I've shared with more than one pastor that they needed to get a life. Some hold on to the insidious idea (and the guilt that comes with it) that if they are not working for the Lord constantly, that they are not pleasing God. I've never felt guilty for taking time for recreation and pleasure apart from my work of pastoring. In fact, I see entertaining friends and neighbors as ministry. Because it is. It's relational. I see recreation with my family as ministry. It's the best way I know to serve them.

Though there are many things in life that I enjoy, there is no passion or love for anything greater than my love for people to come to know Christ. It is that passion that moved me to take my family to Shell Lake and start up a church where there was only one person from Shell Lake who was willing to join us and help us to get started. That person was Linnea Rydberg.

Linnea was an unmarried lady who had taken care of her mother until her passing. She had worked and retired from the Shell Lake Bank after forty-five years there. She was a praying lady and played the piano. She was a member of the Barronett church when we came there, and her piano was the only instrument in use for the worship services.

Linnea told me that she had prayed for many years for a Full Gospel type church to be planted in Shell Lake. I believe that God heard her prayers and when we opened the doors in Shell Lake she was there on her piano to help us lead worship.

Linnea helped us to finance both the church building and the parsonage. She personally paid half of the purchase price of eleven thousand dollars, and we financed the rest at the Shell Lake Bank. She faithfully served as church secretary and treasurer for many years. The church honored Linnea as one of our founders shortly before she passed away.

In 1978, we sold the church and the parsonage to begin building a new facility on five acres of land that we purchased from Wendell Pederson. This is the current site of the Shell Lake Full Gospel Church.

The church building was purchased by the Shell Lake Bank for eleven thousand dollars and donated to the Washburn County Historical Museum. The parsonage was sold to private ownership for twenty-one thousand dollars and has ended up in the hands of the Historical Society and is now a part of the museum.

The Saint John's Lutheran building that was originally built in 1889 had served us well for nine years. We had started with a handful of people with very little knowledge on how to grow a church. God had met with us, and the Holy Spirit moved among us to bring fresh new converts into the church. We were blessed to be part of the revival through the "Jesus movement" and the outpouring of the Holy Spirit in the "charismatic movement."

Many people were getting saved and baptized with the Holy Spirit. We just opened the doors to the Holy Spirit and let the people come in. We grew to the maximum capacity of the building to hold the people. We were then blessed to find five acres of property on the south edge of the city to build a new church complex that would seat three hundred people. We moved into that new facility in 1978. It was a very exciting and happy time in the ministry. Everybody was eager to move forward.

Our beginnings had been very small and at times discouraging since there were some in our community who had been uncomfortable about a new church coming to town. God had promised that He would provide the increase. I've often been asked how I have handled my critics. My answer is, "I have been able to outlast them." I remain free from holding any ill will toward anyone.

Chapter 5
A Surprise Welcome

One of my first contacts in Shell Lake was the mayor of the town. I considered him a nice man, and I think he felt the same about me. I told him of my intentions to begin a new church in the community. His response was unexpected. He stated very matter of fact: "Young man, there are enough churches in town. We really don't need any more." I asked him if he knew how many taverns there were in the community. He responded that there were seven bars in town. I asked him, "How many churches in town?" He told me that there were six churches. Trying to be nice, I countered with "there should be at least as many churches as there are taverns in town." His posture seemed to indicate an attitude of "let's wait and see."

Our next door neighbor to the parsonage was a retired older gentleman who was always kind to my family. He was observant about what was going on at our church and could see that, during our first two years, there was no growth or new people coming. It was always the same few cars that parked in front of the church every week for services.

One day, he confronted me with his concern for my family. He told me that I would not be able to take care of them trying to pastor the church. He stated that it was never going to work. He said that I had a silver tongue and should forget preaching and get a job as a salesman somewhere. I know that he meant well, but didn't understand God's assignment for my life.

Interestingly, five years later that same neighbor approached me again, but this time with a critical complaint. He was upset that cars were parking up and down our street while people walked into the church. It upset him that some cars were blocking his driveway. Hey, good problem! I could take care of that.

But in the early days, we were struggling to get anyone from the community to try our church. It just wasn't happening.

It was evident that people weren't coming to us, so I decided to find ways that I could go to them. I began to visit the local hospital to ask if anyone in there might need a visit or a prayer. The nurses would advise who they thought would be the right ones to see. This presented many opportunities to meet people and build friendships.

One day while visiting the hospital, I saw a man walk across the end of the hallway. I felt a voice in my spirit saying, "Go speak to that man." I stopped by the nurse's station to ask who that man was. They told me his name was Darrell and said that he really needed somebody to talk to him.

When I entered his room, I could see a deep despondency on his face. He said that he knew who I was and told me he had been thinking about contacting me.

Darrell was a bachelor who had been the manager of the hospital clinic for many years. His life had hit bottom from loneliness, and severe depression had pushed him to plan to end his life. His neighbor and close friend intercepted that plan when he arrived at Darrell's home just in time.

I began praying with Darrell, and he surrendered his life to Christ and received the infilling of the Holy Spirit. He was among the first ones to join our church and eventually became our first elder in ministry.

Darrell hired my wife, Linda, at the clinic as a receptionist where she eventually became the assistant manager and stayed on at the clinic for thirty-seven years. She retired in 2013. Darrell passed away of stomach cancer in the late 90's. He was a dear friend and support to our ministry from the beginning of Full Gospel Church.

Another connection to the community was volunteering with the ambulance services to our community. My training, at that time, was limited to advanced first-aid. It didn't feel very competent to meet the kinds of needs that we could be facing when our ambulance arrived at the scene of the call.

My decision to end that brief career came after we had received a call at midnight for an emergency on 7th Avenue. The hospital said it was at an Amundson residence. I knew who the Amundsons were at that address.

My brother, David, who was ten years younger, had moved his wife and four children from Pasadena, California a few months earlier. David had developed a drinking problem, and we thought it would be helpful for him and his family to get a fresh start in Shell Lake. David's wife had developed severe diabetes, along with some depression that resulted from a very cold winter. It was her first winter away from California.

As I pulled the ambulance to the front of their house, I was met by my brother who was yelling at me that his wife was dead. The attendant and I rushed into her room and found her unresponsive, and her body turned dark blue. If anything could be done, it had to be done in seconds. I began clearing her airway while the attendant began compressions. I discovered that her airway was completely blocked, and she was getting no oxygen. At that point, I was lost on what to do. A neighbor, a police officer, and four kids standing in the doorway were all waiting for us to do something. At that moment, I knew it was over without God's help. I opened my mouth and screamed out, "Jesus! Help me!" At that very second, we all heard a loud gasp as air began to flow from my sister-in-law's lungs. We quickly breathed a couple puffs of oxygen into her lungs and rushed her the three blocks to the hospital.

Alcohol and medication are not a good mix, and I spent the rest of the night comforting and praying with my brother.

David moved his family back to California, and after his wife had passed away from complications from her diabetes, he remarried.

I no longer had any interest in ambulatory service so after three years as a volunteer, I resigned. That season was short, but it was educational.

Chapter 6
Jailhouse Religion

I wouldn't want anyone to assume that I never have had personal problems in my life. I have a compulsive personality with a type A temperament. That can be both an asset or a detriment. For me, it has been both.

As an asset, it means that nothing can stop you from getting things accomplished. It means that you never quit or give up. It means that you are always the first batter up and that you will fight like a dog to win. I love competition, but I can't stand losing. Competition keeps life exciting and new adventures are great motivations for me. Frankly, my life is a continual adventure.

The detrimental sides of a compulsive personality are many. Becoming too self-absorbed and narcissistic, being easily distracted, lacking self-discipline, becoming over indulgent, impatience—that's enough for now. I have battled with all of them.

The infilling of the Holy Spirit has helped to balance some of those weaker temperaments into stronger ones. The Holy Spirit bears the fruit of himself which are love, joy, peace, long suffering, gentleness, goodness, faith, meekness, and self-control. This is why the Holy Spirit is so precious to me.

In my late teens, I had begun to rebel against God and against my parent's authority. Satan had tricked me into believing that I was missing out on having more fun in life. Rebellion breaks down all of the safe boundaries and opens wide the doors to sinful behavior. I fell in love with party life and with friends who were running wild. I would fake illness when my parents asked me to go to church and in the middle of the night I would sneak out my downstairs window to join friends who had alcohol and wanted to party.

A compulsive person is not able to stop at one drink, so I usually drank enough to intoxicate me and get home and back through my bedroom window before daybreak. My parents never knew.

I was eighteen years old in my senior year of high school so my friends "used" me to buy beer for them because I was of age. I was busted by the law on two different occasions for contributing to the delinquency of minors and received fines, along with my name written on the front page of the Rice Lake newspapers. What an embarrassment for my parents when my problems were exposed. They began to pray earnestly for me. I just seemed to get worse.

At one high school football game, I got into big trouble. I had been drinking before the game and during the game while sitting as a spectator. We lost the game, and I was upset, so I dropped my empty quart bottle on the ground and kicked it toward the field. I didn't know until the following Monday the result from what I had done. I was called into the superintendent's office, and he was full-blown mad at me. He told me that the bottle I had kicked at the football game had hit him in the back of the head. He punished me by taking away my privileges to play basketball for the first half of my senior year. He dismissed me from all music ensembles that I was scheduled to be in for the rest of the year.

I made the basketball team the second semester and started as point guard on a team that was undefeated until the final state tournament game in Madison, Wisconsin. We lost the state championship game by two points in overtime. It was a great moment for me years later when in 2012, I was honored to be inducted into the Rice Lake Sports Hall of Fame.

In the years following my conversion, I became a friend with that superintendent. I had humbly apologized for the incident, and he remarked that he was pleased to see the change God had made in my life.

There were many embarrassing alcohol-related incidents that exposed the severe problem in my life. I fought hard to keep running away from God, but my parents were relentlessly praying for me. At that point, the compulsive nature and submission to Satan's lies were bent on destroying my life.

The turnaround in my life came at age nineteen when my father had heard that I was at a drinking party in town. I saw him come to the door of the house we were at. I was mortified. My friends saw him too. He opened the door and asked me to come with him. It was only God that could make me agree to go with him. To leave in front of my friends would shame me in their eyes and to not go with my dad would show the ultimate disrespect toward my father in front of my friends. My decision to go with my father that night would be the beginning of the change in my life. I ultimately surrendered to the Lord and felt His complete forgiveness of my sins. I made restitution to some people that I had stolen money and items from as part of my pursuit of a false freedom. I had been forgiven much and God had put a great love and compassion in my heart to help others recover from their failures. I had been genuinely saved!

Jail Chaplain

I was looking for ways to connect with the Shell Lake community and, hopefully, find some prospects to come to our young church. I began to visit the county jail which is located in Shell Lake. I wanted to find opportunities to minister to inmates in the jail.

Sheriff Marvin Anderson and his wife, Dorothy, were in charge of the jail. We developed a good relationship, and he asked if I would like to be deputized as chaplain for the county. I agreed and often would go with him on calls during the evenings. I especially loved the emergency blood runs where Sheriff Anderson would almost bury the needle on the speedometer. The ride was wild.

I would frequently go to the jail to visit with inmates and prayed with many of them to receive Christ. Back then, like today, most inmates are there because of drug use or manufacturing and sales of drugs. Alcohol abuse and related crimes are also strong contributing factors to incarceration. The drug of choice in the 60's and 70's was LSD (also known as acid). It is a dangerous, hallucinatory drug. Reports of people jumping off bridges or out of windows because they thought they could fly were not an exaggeration.

I felt compassion toward the people who were in jail because of drug or alcohol abuse. The sheriff would trust me to take prisoners out of jail on Sunday mornings to come to the church services. There were some on his list that he would not let out. I would go to the jail and unlock the cells of those who were permitted to come with me. This gave us some great opportunities to help heal and restore some broken people. Often my wife would make a lunch and, after the service, we would invite the inmates to eat with us. As long as we demonstrated our trust in them, they would honor that by being trustworthy for us. The Sheriff had set a time of 1:00 p.m. for us to have them back in jail. We did this for several years until new rules were legislated by the state to tighten control of jails and prisoners.

So many times the men and women who were saved from addictions and abuse would do well with their new life in Christ. What we were missing was a ministry that would assist them with recovery and restoration of broken relationships caused by past behavior. A dream had begun in my heart to start praying for a Christian recovery center; a place where recovering addicts could get continued training to grow spiritually and to develop self-confidence for becoming productive in society. A place to be loved and cared for in a non-judgmental environment.

I certainly had no idea how to do that, but I knew that in God's will and in time, He would know how to make it happen. God can remain silent for a long time when you feel like you need instant answers. But His thoughts and His ways are very different than ours. He always hears us when we pray, but I have learned that when He answers our prayers, they are always answered right on time. His time.

His plan was already in process.

Chapter 7
A Place for Compassion

In 1987, a young man came to Shell Lake from Rockford, Illinois with plans to take a break from an alcoholic lifestyle. His lifestyle had squeezed him into the need to look for a respite from alcohol abuse. His name is Reg Myers.

Reg is a grandson to Harvey and Mary Myers, who had lived on the Red Cedar River in Rice Lake when I was growing up there. I was very close friends with the Myers family and especially with two of the boys, whom I spent time hunting and fishing with. Reg's mother was the oldest of Harvey and Mary's twelve children, and I do remember occasions when he and his brother Rod and their parents would visit Reg's grandparents in Rice Lake. I can't remember Reg very well, but I do remember his brother Rod who was crippled in both legs. Rod would scoot around in his braces and tried to stay involved with whatever we older boys were doing. When Reg's grandpa Harvey died, I was asked to sing at his funeral. His grandmother Mary attended our church for a time before she passed away. I officiated at her funeral service.

When Reg came to Shell Lake, he moved into his uncle Bob and Marilyn Erwin's home intending to stay there for a short time to dry out and then return to his hometown of Rockford.

Marilyn Erwin is the youngest daughter of Harvey and Mary Myers, and so she is Reg's aunt. Bob and Marilyn have been at the Full Gospel Church since moving to Shell Lake in 1980. Bob has served as an elder in the church for over twenty years.

When Reg stopped at the Erwin's for help and support, he received much more than he would have thought or asked for. Bob was in the logging business and put Reg to work with him. Bob told Reg that the only help he could offer for his alcohol problem was that he would have to surrender his life to Christ as his Lord and Savior.

Reg made his decision to serve Christ and began to attend Full Gospel Church regularly. He soon began dating a young lady in the church. Her name was Dawn Manning. Reg and Dawn fell in love, and it was my pleasure to perform their wedding in 1988.

For the first ten years of their married life, Reg didn't seem to show much interest in spiritual things. He would sit in the back of the church and observe everything that was taking place in the services. But God was speaking to his heart about consecrating his life totally to Him.

Reg had been inactive in the church and was becoming more dissatisfied in his spirit and made a decision to pursue God's purpose for his life. He would take his Bible and go downstairs in his house very early in the morning to spend an hour or two seeking the Holy Spirit for direction in his life.

For over three months, Reg practiced this routine every day, consecrating himself to meet with God. When he came upstairs each day after praying, Dawn would ask him if he had experienced anything. Each time he would tell her that nothing unusual happened.

On January 4th, 1997, something unusual did happen in that prayer chamber that Reg visited every morning. Reg stated that "a warm, bright light appeared while I was praying and saturated my whole being." He was filled with the Holy Spirit, and when he came upstairs, his wife didn't have to ask him if anything unusual happened. She knew from looking at him that God had met him that morning.

Reg's life was clearly transformed that day. He came to me and stated that all he wanted to do was to serve in any capacity that was available. He wanted to totally serve God. He also told me that he felt God had spoken clearly to him that he would become a pastor.

At that time our custodians in the church had resigned so we asked if he would be willing to take on that role. Reg had developed his own painting business and painted homes in the Shell Lake area. He donated many additional hours in doing a great service to the church by taking care of all the church facilities. He did a great job.

In 1998, Reg started up a men's prayer ministry every Tuesday morning at 6:30 a.m. He has consistently opened the church for men's prayer each week, and this ministry continues as of this writing. Reg Myers also prepared himself for ministry by continuing his education and receiving his Bachelor Degree and Master's Degree in Biblical Studies. He was added to our church staff and eldership full time in 2002.

Also in 1998, a man named Pat Dixon came into our lives. Pat had given his heart to serve the Lord after a lifetime of addictions and dysfunctions. We can't begin to sort out Pat's life except to say that he had been through over forty institutions for attempts at rehabilitation. Pat was in his late fifties and was very cooperative in helping us to better understand those with addictions similar to his. Pat said the only thing that he had ever found to free him from alcohol and drugs was the relationship that he had found with Jesus Christ. He knew he had been forgiven. The day that we baptized Pat in water was another life-changing moment for Pat. He had a deep fear of water that was caused by a service-related incident where some military members had fallen into the sea. He had tried to reach his hand to grasp them, but they were pulled away from him and drowned. He had become extremely fearful of water.

Pat told me that as soon as he came up from the waters of baptism, he had no more fears and later told me that he had no more nightmares from that incident. God had freed him.

Reg and Pat began to work together and pray together about what could be done to provide a long-term recovery facility for men who wanted to serve Christ but had been captive to drugs and alcohol for a lengthy time. Many of them had served time in jails or prison. We opened up the church parsonage temporarily as a place of ministry for men. We knew if we could hold onto these men through a longer period of recovery, that there would be better success in growing their faith and restoring their broken souls. We needed to build fences at the top of the cliff to keep them from falling to the bottom again.

Pat Dixon was our catalyst. He knew the nature of these men and the kind of stinking thinking they were accustomed to. When combined with Reg's compassion as a result of his own critical problems early in life, these two men were key to implementing a new ministry called Compassion Connection.

The church parsonage was available for short-term housing and even though space was available, it would be four months before the first client would come in. His name was Craig. This was in 2001.

Pat Dixon and Reg Myers would add another key person to the Compassion Ministry. He was Tom Terrill, who had come to the Lord and became part of Full Gospel Church as a result of his son coming to Christ through the Compassion Connection ministry. His son had become a teenage addict to drugs and alcohol and had spent time in prison for crimes related to his abuse. When Tom saw the results of Christ's power to change his son, it turned his own heart to God.

Tom has become very active with Compassion Connection and has become an official chaplain of the Washburn County Sheriff's Department. He works actively with jail inmates and successfully leads many of them to salvation in Christ. He is a key resource involved in bringing men through a three to six-month recovery at the Compassion Center.

The Compassion Center

In 2009, God opened up a large home at the Northwest edge of the Shell Lake community. It was owned by Jerry Curtis from Shell Lake, and he leased it to the church for one year. This gave some time to have the property rezoned by the city to house up to ten people in the facility. In 2010, the church purchased the property from the Curtis family and the realization of an old dream, that I received over forty years earlier, was born. A place to provide ongoing care for recovering broken lives of men in crises with addictions and loss. We now had a place with an overseer to the Compassion Ministry, my associate pastor, Reg Myers.

The name of the facility is known as "The Compassion Center."

Though Pat Dixon would have loved to have been a part of the new center, he did not live to see it come to pass. He was an important part of the ministry, and we all loved him deeply. He was scheduled to be at a Tuesday evening Compassion Ministry meeting but did not show up. Reg and I, along with Tom Terrill, went to his home and found him deceased lying in his bed. He had overdosed on his prescription of OxyContin which he used to relieve pain. We had prayed with him during men's prayer that morning and I had met with him in my office at 8:00 a.m. We discussed the slurring in his speech, and I told him that he was taking too many pain pills and needed to rest that day. I did not know that when he went home to lay down that he would never get up again. It was a sad day for all of us who loved Pat Dixon. The Compassion Center is dedicated in honor of Pat Dixon who God brought to us to teach us that God values every human life, no matter what form it comes in.

Bob and Jeanine Solum were asked to serve as in-house directors of Compassion Center. They accepted and moved from Rice Lake to Shell Lake and into the Center in 2013. This is a special couple in my life. In Bob's early years I was involved in helping him with his breakthrough journey to freedom from alcohol. We have been very close since.

God has used Bob to help restore and encourage many men to rise up to a higher and more wholesome level of faith in their lives. His compassion qualifies him as a director of the recovery center. There are many men who will attest to that.

I am so grateful to know that the ministry of compassion to restore men with various addictions is in such capable hands as Reg Myers, Tom Terrill, and Bob Solum and those guys who work with him.

Chapter 8
The Timely Vision

Linda and I lived in the parsonage next door to the small former Lutheran Church building while we were trying to plant a new congregation. Part of our compensation was living rent-free. The rest was twenty-five dollars a week provided by the fifteen members who attended every week.

I was twenty-seven years old, at the time, and provided the rest of the income we needed by driving to Rice Lake every weekday to my job. Linda left her job as a telephone operator in Rice Lake to take care of our three small children. She learned to sew and helped our budget by making the children's clothes and making several polyester suits for me to wear in the pulpit. She looked after our family needs, I juggled my time between my secular job and running to hospitals, nursing homes, jail ministry, and finding time to study and prepare for preaching three times weekly.

The transition to Shell Lake was more wearing on my wife because my daily absence for work and ministry which resulted in a lack of quality time with my family. I tried to justify that absence by telling them how busy I was in ministry for the Lord and how I needed to work to take care of my family. But, God only gives us a small window of time in our life for raising children. Those are the most rewarding and pleasurable years. To think that anything else we do is more important than spending time with our family is just plain ignorant and selfish.

It took a severe crisis in our marriage relationship to bring me to my senses and move me to finally and seriously sort out my priorities between the ministry, my job, and my family. Linda graciously accepted my appeal for more time to turn things around. I couldn't see my own problems so I couldn't change myself. I needed to become broken in my spirit and ask God to change me. I knew that if I lost my family, I would also lose the ministry God had given me. God helped me to make slow changes in my priorities, forgave my selfishness, and ultimately renewed my marriage. He gave me a wife who is gracious, kind, and patient. Her loyalty has been a mainstay for me and has helped me to be a faithful husband and friend through the years. Of course, there have been adjustments from time to time on both of our parts. Both of us have had to work to get it right.

We had been in Shell Lake for three years before God gave us our first convert. I was in my study on a Saturday morning when a man knocked on our door asking to see me. He introduced himself as Roy Slater and asked me to help him. His wife had left him with five children because of an alcoholic problem she had. He did not want to give her up. Roy had heard me share a brief message at the annual Memorial Day service in Shell Lake. Something I had said had stuck with him, so he thought that maybe I could help him. Roy was a member of the city council and was known in the community because he had lived here his entire life.

I befriended him and shared with him what Christ had done to save him and his wife. He prayed with me to receive Christ. I told him that I would contact him that week. I was surprised to see him later that same afternoon when he again came to the house, this time bringing his wife with him. He had gone to see her, and she had noticed there was something different about him when she saw him. She asked him what had happened, and he told her. He asked if she would come to meet me. She agreed, and here they were together. She asked me what I had done to her husband. We all sat down, and I shared God's plan for forgiveness with her. She believed and received the Lord. The next morning was Sunday and what joy it was to see Roy and his wife Gladys walk hand in hand into the church. I had just witnessed our first converts in our ministry in Shell Lake. Roy and Gladys were baptized and began bringing four of their five children to church. Three of their children were teenagers and came because of the change they had seen in their parent's lives.

The amazing grace of God concerning this family is that eventually all five of their children became born-again, spirit-filled believers. Each one of them became ministers at different points in time. The oldest, Roy Jr., ministered in Florida; Ted is currently ministering in Ohio; Peggy served with mission works in Japan and Columbia; Nancy served as a worship director in Montana, and Dan is the youth director and now working with young families and world missions on staff in Full Gospel Church. In the early years, Gladys played guitar for worship and Ted was our first church drummer. He went on to play drums for the Chancellors before attending Bible college in North Dakota. I will always be grateful that the Lord brought the Slater family to us. It started our move forward.

Our small community took notice of the change in the Slater family, and people began to hear about their involvement in the church. I don't mean that suddenly the community started filling up our pews.

We were in our fourth year of ministry, and the growth that we had hoped for was not yet taking place. I was young, eager, and impatient. I think my prayers for God to move upon the ministry in Shell Lake started to turn into whining. I was struggling with God. He had called me, why was He waiting so long to bless me?

One cold night in January I went to the church to teach in our midweek service. I mean it was cold. Somewhere in the minus 20's or 30's. Below zero! I can't blame people for not showing up for service that night. I was going to close up the church and walk home when I felt an urgency to go to the platform and pray. At first, my prayers were of the whining and complaining type. I wasn't getting anywhere and only felt more discouraged.

46

I remember feelings of desperation coming upon me, and I began to weep uncontrollably. I emptied out every feeling inside of me, including thoughts about quitting our ministry in Shell Lake if God didn't do something to show His favor.

It went from complaining to repenting to deep intercession, where I lost track of time. I only knew that I had found God's holy presence, and I needed to remain in it as long as possible.

Sometime during this spiritual encounter, I saw the inside of the small sanctuary completely filled with people from front to back and the little balcony also full of people. The people all had their arms extended in praise toward heaven. Everyone's faces looked happy and full of love. A voice spoke into my spirit and said, "This house shall be full, and the people will be filled with praises unto the Lord!" That was it. The picture was gone. But I will never forget its vividness. It seemed so real.

The scripture tells us that God gives visions to young men and dreams to old men. I am now past being a visionary person but do receive an occasional dream from the Lord. We had been in a season of dryness and unfruitfulness and were waiting on the Lord for a breakthrough.

The next five years of ministry was the most exciting and fruitful years of ministry. With the help of the sovereign Jesus Movement and an outpouring of the Holy Spirit upon every denomination known as the Charismatic Movement, we enjoyed unprecedented growth in the church.

The Jesus Movement was attracting young people all over the nation. Worship music style completely changed, and young people were drawn to Christian rock-style music that was high in volume and praise to the Lord. This was the beginning when hymnals were being replaced with choruses. Later in the 90's, the use of new technology created transparencies on screens where we read the songs on the screen. There were no notes to follow. I felt that our worship team has always been on the cutting-edge of good worship. As worship styles have changed, their heart for worship and love to worship has never changed.

The newest technology is PowerPoint slides projected onto a screen and most music being sung for worship is contemporary style. I willingly adapt to every style because I love to worship God. We saw many young people in the area truly converted to Jesus and openly share their love for Him to one another. This movement was a counterpart to the Hippie Movement which took place during and after the Vietnam War.

We opened the church to receive this new generation of culture style that differed from our status quo traditional church style. We learned not to judge people by their outward appearance, but by the love in their hearts. So many of these Jesus people eventually became pastors, leaders, missionaries, and active church members supporting new testament churches that were springing up all over the nation. God was good to raise up spiritual leaders across the nation who were gifted teachers to bring maturity and godly order to this new generation from the post-Vietnam era. It was a much-needed renewal that stemmed the tide of anarchy and runaway rebellion that gripped our nation.

The Charismatic Movement differed from the Jesus Movement in relation to the supernatural. God was pouring out His Holy Spirit upon traditional denominational churches across the nation and other parts of the world. The supernatural gifts of the Holy Spirit were bringing miracles of healing and other power gifts into the church. Gifts of prophecy and the gifts of speaking in tongues, often called glossolalia, was being experienced by people in all denominations, which had been primarily practiced by the Pentecostal churches. It was called a Third Wave movement by the media. I personally attended some of these meetings where nuns and priests worshiped with Lutherans and Methodists at worship venues, with hands raised to the father and prayers being prayed in the spirit with unknown tongues. I witnessed physical healings and miracles over people who were prayed for by Lutheran Pastors and Roman Catholic Priests. I saw the joy of the Lord and all the glory given to Jesus. God used the movement to shake up traditional churches. He shook up religious pride that tried to contain God in religious forms and ceremonies. These movements were totally sovereign from God.

Full Gospel Church opened its doors to embrace the supernatural and God began to bring in denominational people whose hearts were hungry to experience God's power. The spirit of the church came alive, and faith rose to a new level continually. People who were touched by the Holy Spirit were getting saved and baptized in water. Many came in from other nearby communities, and we were enjoying an increase both numerically and financially.

Evangelist Kenneth Knight was one man that God used to help the growth of the church. He had a powerful gift of "word of knowledge" and incredible faith for healing. We saw many miracles and healings on several occasions when we had him come.

People were drawn to the church by the authentic demonstration of God's power. It was a good period for the church during the mid and late 1970s.

On Easter Sunday in 1977, we were doing a live radio broadcast from the church during the service. A prophecy came forth during the worship. We now had an orchestra of several instruments leading the worship. After the prophecy which contained an encouraging message from the Holy Spirit, the people were all standing with their hands raised to the father. I noticed that every pew was packed with people and that the church balcony was full as well. Everyone looked happy, and God's love filled their hearts. It was an incredible sight, and I began to cry because this was the exact scene that I had seen five years earlier on that below zero night while praying all alone as I laid on the church platform. It was déjà vu for me. The vision had been fulfilled literally before my eyes on that Easter Sunday. We were part of God's divine destiny to establish a New Testament Church in a small community.

Another transition was in the making. We needed to expand and increase into a larger facility. But first, we needed the property to build a new facility. We asked God to show us where He wanted us to move. Again, He would be faithful to lead us.

Chapter 9
Time to Build

A couple who came to the church early on was Buck and Violet Krakhau. They were older, but God was very real to them, and they were very faithful every week to attend every service. At one time, Violet had the distinction of being a licensed fishing guide in northwest Wisconsin. She really knew the Shell Lake waters, having fished them since she was a small girl. When I came to Shell Lake, she owned her own resort on the lake. I will just say that I learned a few of her secrets for fishing walleyes and, as a result, have had some great success on the lake over the years. Her daughter, Carolyn, was saved about the same time or just before her mother and step-father. This was in 1972. Carolyn was a great witness of her faith and led other family members, friends, and neighbors to the Lord. Many of them joined the church. I mention Carolyn because she is currently the longest standing member of Full Gospel Church and continues to attend faithfully every Sunday.

Buck was like an adopted father to me. We spent a lot of time together in the early years of our ministry. He loved God, and he loved the church. I counted on his help often. He eventually developed an inner ear problem and finally Alzheimer's, which took his life.

Buck and I often discussed plans to build a new church facility. We would sit at his dining room table and draw up plans of what we thought it should look like. This was in 1977. We came up with a plan that we thought would work whenever we the opportunity to build a church. It was only a rough drawn description, but we had fun with it.

In 1977, our church board and elders agreed that it was time to build. The congregation voted to go ahead. So, the church purchased five acres of property on the south edge of town that bordered Highway 63. We purchased it from Wendell Pederson for eight thousand dollars.

We hired Bill Turner from Hayward to design the plans and get state approvals for the project. Bill was a certified architect and took on the project himself. Buck and I gave him the plans we had drawn on his table, and he used them as an outline for his approved draft. When the church was finally completed in 1978, it was built according to the same design that we had originally drawn on Buck's living room table. As an added blessing, Bill Turner donated all of his time in drawing up the architectural plans and getting approval from the state. He saved us approximately twelve thousand dollars. We all were very grateful to Bill for his generous support.

We knew that the finances needed to help us get started with the building would depend on the sale of the old church building and the parsonage in which my family and I had been living for nine years. We asked God to give us buyers for both buildings. We had no idea how these buildings would sell.

When the land was purchased to build a new church building, Linda and I asked for and received from the church a half-acre of the property to give us some equity for financing our own home. We had lived next door to the church for nine years, and we were willing to continue living next to the new church. We did that for the next twenty-two years.

With help from some of the trades people in the church who donated much of their own labor, we were blessed to be able to get enough equity to get a mortgage on our very first home. The house was completed in 1978, and we moved from the old parsonage into our new home.

Before we had begun the building of the church, the Shell Lake Bank president had notified us that we had been approved for the construction loan for the church. We went ahead with the excavation, and the foundation of blocks and cement work was completed. The materials from the lumber company in Spooner had been delivered on site, and we had used the money we had on hand to pay for the foundation. I went to the bank to ask them to go ahead and put one hundred thousand dollars into the church account. That's when I received a shocking surprise. The bank president called me into his office and explained to me that the bank board had requested that the church declare a larger reserve of liquid assets than we had available for them to approve the loan.

Darrell Bailey was with me, and we both sat surprised since we had been told that the loan would be no problem. Now we were in a fix because the lumber company wanted their payment of several thousand dollars, and we had no money to pay them. We did not have the liquid assets they requested. We had to do something else.

The elders suggested that we try the bank of Spooner. Darrell and I proceeded to talk to them. They were more than eager to grant us a loan for the amount we needed. Consequently, the church would have to transfer its accounts to the Spooner Bank. We were grateful for their support.

Shortly after losing the church account at the Shell Lake Bank, the bank board made a nice gesture to the community and county by purchasing our old church building and donating it to the county Historical Society. They gave us the amount of money that the church had paid for both the church and parsonage nine years earlier. We were grateful to the Shell Lake Bank for a building that we foresaw as improbable for us to sell.

A few years later, the church transferred its accounts back to the Shell Lake Bank, and they have served us well for many years. The new Full Gospel Church was dedicated to God's service in June of 1978. I remember our first wedding took place on the second weekend after we had held our first service. The church was not finished, and the fellowship hall needed much work to be ready for the reception. Mike Spears and Kathy Crosby were the first couple to be married in the church, and they and the people of the congregation worked frantically all week to get everything in place. They did it, and Mike and Kathy had a beautiful wedding. They raised four daughters who are grown and married. All of them serve the Lord. Kathy came to the Lord during the Jesus Movement. The Spears family have been a great help to the church for many years.

The present home of Shell Lake Full Gospel Church.

Our children grew up in the home we built next to the church. Though they lived in a glass house for all the community to observe as preacher's kids, Linda and I are eternally grateful that they honored us by their obedience and sound character that was above reproach to the church and the community.

Teresa graduated from college with a business and accounting degree. Brent received his master's degree in business and Angel received a degree in communications.

Currently, Teresa is the church bookkeeper. Brent lives in Dallas, Texas and is the Human Resource Talent Acquisition Director for Dell Corporation. Angel is a director of business development of a tech company in Blaine, Minnesota. She still plays volleyball and coaches girls volleyball in Minnesota.

When we moved from the old church parsonage to our new home on the south edge of Shell Lake, there were only two other homes newly built in that area. The neighbor's corn fields and all of the area north of our former home has been developed into scores of homes. To the south, there is the Shell Lake Junior and Senior High School with track and ball fields which border the church property.

We had purchased a three-acre lot on Ripley Lake eight miles east of Shell Lake in 1995. Our hope was to build a home there sometime. Glenn Knoop was a good friend in the church who helped me clear the land of trees to give enough space to build a home. Jim Leonard, who was a special confidant to me and blessing to the church, helped me to measure up the setbacks from the lake and mark corners to where our new house would sit.

Jim and his wife, Gladys, had received a spiritual awakening with the Holy Spirit in the church and made their move from a denominational church in Spooner to Full Gospel Church in Shell Lake. Jim had retired from the Wisconsin State Highway Department and took his time to travel with me to counsel and pray with people in the surrounding communities. I depended on his help, and he always responded to serve wherever he could.

He battled with prostate cancer for seventeen years, but it never daunted him or prevented him from assisting Pastor Reg Myers or myself whenever we would call for his help. Jim was a caring supporter of our Compassion Ministry and kept us all encouraged to keep going when things were difficult. He was our right-hand person for many years. A strong financial support, Jim was loyal and faithful to the church unto the end of his life. He passed into the heavens in 2004. We still miss him.

Linda and I sold our house next to the church in 1999 and began to build our new house on Ripley Lake. We completed the house which was built by Andy Falstad and moved in after our missions conference at the end of October. Andy Falstad served in the church on the worship team. He formerly traveled with a Christian rock group known as Petra. Andy was the lighting director for them. He did a great job in building our house.

Transition means "change." It is evident that much change has taken place since the church moved from in town Shell Lake to the outside edge of the city. Much more change is to come.

Chapter 10
My Pastor's Vision

Shortly before my pastor C.L. Warner passed away in 1980, he shared with me a vision God had given him. He laid out for me a map of northern Wisconsin and told me that there would be three churches established in the area which would result from his ministry in Rice Lake.

He told me that Shell Lake would be one of the church plants and that two more would be planted, one north of Shell Lake somewhere near Hayward, Wisconsin and another one near the Turtle Lake area. I marked that in my memory and wondered how that would ever happen. Only one of the three churches that he had seen in his vision had been established. Pastor Warner did not live to see the fulfillment of the vision as he died from heart failure in 1980. It was a huge loss in my life since it was he who had discipled me and gave me my first years of training in the ministry. I am indebted to his love and mentorship.

Pastor Warner's son, Timothy, had just graduated from International Bible College in San Antonio, Texas and I brought him to Shell Lake to help with our youth ministry. My wife had introduced him to a young lady who had attended our church and had graduated from college with a teacher's degree. They fell in love, and I performed their wedding in 1981. Tim's wife, Sandy, took a job as an elementary teacher in Shell Lake. They lived in Shell Lake for three years.

I had received a call from an architect in Hayward, whose name was Bill Turner. He and a small group were meeting in his home as a prayer and praise group. The group was part of a historic Church of Christ in Hayward. Bill had invited me to come and teach them about the Holy Spirit and so I went to become acquainted with them. After a couple of meetings, I asked them if I could invite Tim Warner to teach them. They agreed and soon he was able to find favor with them.

I made an appointment for Tim and me to meet with the elderly pastor of the church to inform him of our intent. We wanted him to know that we did not intend to proselytize people from his congregation. He received us well and told us that he didn't know how to handle these "charismatic" people that were attending his congregation. It was only a couple months later that he called me and told me he was resigning from his ministry and asked me if Tim Warner would be interested in pastoring the church. Tim and I agreed that if his elders were willing to adopt a new constitution and by-laws, and give authority for Tim to be in charge as pastor, we would consider the offer. His elders agreed, and the process for the transition from a traditional Church of Christ into an independent

Full Gospel autonomous church began. It was not an easy transition. Making the change from a board controlled congregation to a pastor/elders controlled one was difficult for everyone.

The church was set in place with a new leader and a new government. Tim and his wife, Sandy, moved from Shell Lake to Hayward, and they named the new church Northern Lights Christian Center. The building was small. Eventually, God gave them growth to where they were able to build a larger center for worship and to develop a Christian school, which continues to grow.

This was the second of the three churches that Tim's father had received in a vision which he had shared with me before he died.

Dr. Tim Warner and I both have been licensed with the International Ministerial Association through all of our years in ministry. Tim has served as the chairman of the general board of the I.M.A. for several years and has helped to successfully move the I.M.A. forward through his innovative ideas and vision to build healthy ministries. I have always been considered his pastor and our relationship has remained at the deepest level of love and trust.

In the late 1990's, God began to speak into my heart concerning the people from the Turtle Lake area who had been attending our church. Several families traveled thirty to forty miles each week to attend our services. They were very committed, and I had grown close to them as a pastor and friend. Among them were Bob and Sharon Orf and their four children whom we had become close to. Bob owned a successful business in Turtle Lake and was well-known in that community. They were faithful supporters of the church.

There were no evangelical or charismatic churches in Turtle Lake, and the number of people who attended our church from that area was significant enough for an evangelical church to be established there. I knew that God would have to raise up a strong leader and that the test of His will would be for the people to be united in supporting a church plant there. Some of the people in Turtle Lake had been praying for God's will concerning a new church plant.

In 1998, I was asked to speak at a missionary convention at Destiny Church in San Antonio, Texas. This church was formerly known as Revival Temple, which was founded in the 1950's by Pastor John Bell.

I included John Bell in this book because of his great influence in my life as a spiritual father and mentor. He and his wife Ruth had spent several years in Japan as missionaries before moving back to San Antonio. I had become acquainted with the Bells when he was a guest minister at my home church in Rice Lake when I was a teenager. My pastor, Caleb Warner, had him speak at his first small mission conference.

When I first entered into the ministry, we started a mission program to help with financial support for missionaries. We invited a few missionaries who had graduated from International Bible College in San Antonio. Some of those names of missionaries who visited us in our early ministry were Russell and Lydia Chorpening, Chuck and Joan Dewing, Sheldon and Elaine Dwyer, Johnny Eils, Lester and Peggy Seiler, Larry Russell, Jerry and Betty McSorley and Frank Holmes. Some of these we have continued monthly support for over forty-five years.

In October 1986, we started our first World Missions Conference in Shell Lake. We invited missionaries who we knew and had helped support to join us for the four-day event. That was the beginning of what has become an internationally known World Missions Conference, and it was kicked off by an excellent pastor and missionary statesman, Pastor John Bell.

It was after I had spoken in San Antonio that I was approached by a couple from Albuquerque, New Mexico. They introduced themselves as Ken and Connie Mandley. Ken was a retired Air Force officer and was serving on the staff of a large Assembly of God church in Albuquerque. Ken told me that he and his wife had grown up near Madison, Wisconsin and both of them had graduated from Bible college before Ken joined the Air Force. We had a brief conversation, and he asked if we could continue our conversation over phone calls. I agreed, and we did continue to visit on the phone several times over the next several years. Ken stated that he had felt a pastoral call and wondered if I knew of any churches in Wisconsin that might need a pastor.

In 2004, I set up a meeting with Ken and Connie at an I.M.A. National Conference in Rockford, Illinois. We discussed the possibility of planting a new church in

Turtle Lake. The first step was to meet with some of the members of our church who were from the Turtle Lake area. Ken and Connie spent a few months in Shell Lake as we worked together to build relationships and gain the confidence of the people in Turtle Lake. It gave them time to pray over the area and to confirm to both parties that this was God's plan and God's time. God brought His confirmation to begin this new work in Turtle Lake.

The Shell Lake church blessed and released the families from that area to leave us and establish what is now known as Grace Community Church in Turtle Lake, Wisconsin. Our church elders commissioned and ordained Ken and Connie Mandley to become pastors over the new congregation. We agreed to provide a covering over them through our eldership.

Grace Church first held their services in the Turtle Lake high school commons each Sunday for the first seven years. They began to grow and built a new facility in 2012 and added the second of three phases to their total plan in 2015. God has blessed them.

The church in Shell Lake was obedient to follow through with what God had put in our hearts to do. At first, it seemed a costly obedience for the church when we realized an immediate drop in our attendance from those who left for the Turtle Lake church. We also noticed a drop in the finances because most of those families were faithful givers.

But we were investing in expanding God's kingdom unselfishly. God would take care of us. We all felt a new joy that this transition of helping to plant a new church had pleased the Lord. The path to true happiness is through giving. Jesus said that if our seed (money, people) is planted into good soil, it will return as much as "hundredfold" (Luke 8:8, author's paraphrase). And he said, "Give, and you will receive. Your gift will return to you in full—pressed down, shaken together to make room for more, running over, and poured into your lap. The amount you give will determine the amount you get back" (Luke 6:38 NLT).

Our congregation had emptied out so we could make room for more. We had not given our weakest or least committed families. We had given our strongest and most faithful. It is the sacrifice of obedience that is most acceptable to God. Obedience always offers its best.

Within six months after we had released those who helped to start the new church in Turtle Lake, God had measured back to us. We had noticed that our numbers in attendance had exceeded our losses, and the church budget income had increased above what had been before those folks leaving. The kingdom of God was expanding. I think that God was happy, and so were we.

The church in Turtle Lake had been the culmination of the vision of three churches that my pastor had described to me shortly before he died. He saw them connected indirectly to his own ministry in Rice Lake where he had planted the church that I was saved and grew up in. He had taken much time to prepare me and pray with me to be launched into ministry. He had graciously released me to begin my first pastorate in Barronett in 1966. My uncle and spiritual father, my mentor, Pastor C.L. Warner made an investment into my life that continues to produce kingdom results nearly fifty years later.

It is such a great feeling to have been part of God's purpose and destiny and to watch His hand accomplish the counsel of His will in His own time.

To every minister who has felt discouragement at times and have thoughts of leaving the ministry, let me say this: discouragement is only a test (especially on Monday mornings). The test of discouragement is intended more to make you into of a man of God than it is to make you successful in the ministry. God is only after your obedience. Quitting must never be an option. It's all about obedience. Apart from obedience to God, there is no success! Obedience really is—the bottom line.

Chapter 11
Adjusting to Changes

When we first started our ministry in Shell Lake we were operating on very limited funds. The church income was just enough to pay the mortgage and utilities. I received twenty-five dollars from the church per week. The church provided us the parsonage and paid our utilities. We were occasionally blessed with contributions of groceries and small financial gifts.

After moving to Shell Lake, I continued to work for Brown Sales in Rice Lake for three more years, driving each way five days a week. In 1972 at the age of thirty, I left Brown Sales having worked there for nine years and stepped into the ministry full time.

Linda was staying at home caring for our three small children. She helped to stretch our meager budget with her creativity. She took sewing classes and learned how to make clothes for the children, many times making outfits for all three children from the same material. She had the kids looking good all dressed alike. She also learned how to make men's suits and she made several dress ones for me from polyester material she found. They looked great, and they fit me perfectly. Linda went to work at the Shell Lake Clinic after all of our children had started school. She worked part time during the summer months.

Our early years in Shell Lake were years of many adjustments. It was an adjustment for us to manage the family needs with less income. It was an adjustment to leave our family and lifelong friends in Rice Lake to come to a community where we knew no one. It was an adjustment for my wife and family not to have me home during the day and to be gone most evenings doing ministry work. I did not do well at prioritizing time with my children, justifying myself as being too busy doing God's work. The lessons I learned from failing to minister to my own family were nearly very costly ones.

I did not recognize the signs of depression and discouragement that was building up in my wife. I thought that everything was going well for us and that Linda was handling the adjustments well. I was so busy and on the run all the time that I didn't take time or give thought to her feelings or concerns.

Linda had to finally resort to shock treatment to get my undivided attention. She told me that she was going to take the children and move out for a while and go be with her family. When I finally realized her seriousness on the matter, my mind went numb. I had been deceived into believing that we could not have any problems in our marriage. We were Christians. We were in love. We were building a new church for God's glory. How could it possibly come to this? I had always believed that a minister who failed in his marriage would also fail in his ministry. And now I would have to come to grips with my own beliefs and failures.

The first thing we did was to set everything else aside so we could rebuild our communication. I appealed to Linda for more time before she carried out her decision. I knew that there were changes I would have to make, but didn't trust myself that I could keep them. She did give me more time, and the first thing I did was to get alone with God and ask for His help to change me. Slowly and prayerfully, I began to feel God's favor and receive my wife's favor. God restored us and restored our trust toward each other. God had put us together from high school sweethearts to being married for over fifty-three years at this writing.

Most of our years together and our service in the ministry have been filled with bright days. The joy of the Lord has been our strength. I've learned that adjustments are made easier the more we are mature and come through experiences in life.

In 1975 Linda was pregnant with our fourth child. The pregnancy was going well, and the baby was due in the first week of June. On a Sunday evening June 8th, I had just returned home from a Lowell Lundstrom crusade in Rice Lake. Linda was overdue and not feeling well, so she had stayed home. She was scheduled to have the baby by caesarean on Monday morning. While she was in delivery, I stayed downstairs to visit with the hospital administrator. The door opened to our room, and the doctor burst in, and I could see on his face that something was wrong. He was shaking and told me that something terrible had happened. My baby was dead, and my wife was in critical condition. Something indeed had gone terribly wrong. This was the darkest day of my life.

Our plan had been to have our baby by caesarean section since Linda had had trouble with natural delivery of our other children. For our last child, she was overdue and without our knowing it, she was developing toxemia, which resulted in the baby dying in the womb the day before her surgery. No one was prepared for what happened. The baby was gone, and the nurses were working feverishly to reduce Linda's body temperature which was staying at one hundred seven degrees. She was full of poison and hanging in the balance of life and death. We had just lost our baby, and I just knew that I couldn't take the loss of my wife. I got alone in a room and poured out my heart to God to save my wife. I remember even the nurses were saying prayers for her. By the end of the day, her temperature dropped, and she was out of danger.

God sometimes permits us to go through humbling circumstances to help us become aware of some needed adjustments we must make in our lives. I had been so confident and secure in myself, and so on the go with my plans and ambitions that I had neglected the attention and care of the most important people in my life. Now I had almost lost my wife twice. Once by a near divorce, and now by near death. These were wake-up moments for me. I needed to make adjustments early in the ministry which ultimately would affect those who followed our ministry through the years. God has always given me a healthy fear of the Lord. There is wisdom that comes with that. The battle for me has been to always remain humble in my heart so that God will receive all the glory for anything that He has done through us. A prayer that I often ask God for is in Psalm 36:11 (KJV), "Let not the foot of pride come against me, and let not the hand of the wicked drive me away." Pride has taken many good men down. The scripture says that "pride goes before destruction" (Proverbs 16:18 NKJV).

God has blessed me with many honors and rewards for which I do not feel worthy. Some perhaps will be recorded in eternity while no doubt many others will vanish away when life is over. Whatever is lost or gained, my hope is that God will receive the glory due Him and will judge his servant to have been faithful.

My wife and I recovered from the loss of our baby in time. The first year was a battle for her with some depression and feelings of loss. We never blamed anyone or even God for our loss. I developed a deeper respect for my wife and a greater realization of how fragile life is. Our three children grew up to make us proud of their commitment to serving the Lord in such a way that their friends gave them much respect.

Teresa, our oldest, was born with slight cerebral palsy. She overcame some limitations and played volleyball in school. She earned a certification in accounting at a vocational college in Rice Lake and is employed by Full Gospel Church as Bookkeeper. She and her husband, Gary have raised three children. One son and two daughters.

Our son Brent graduated from Shell Lake High School and was the president of his senior class. He earned a business degree from Northwestern College in Roseville, Minnesota. He received his M.B.A. from St. Thomas University in St. Paul, Minnesota. Brent and his wife, Melanie, raised two sons and live in Dallas, Texas. Their youngest son, Luke, was born with special needs. He was born with Spina Bifida and partial paralysis. Later he was diagnosed as being on the Autism spectrum. They have provided the best care for Luke and will continue their care of him the rest of his life. Brent is Vice President of talent acquisition at Dell, Inc. He and his wife Melanie teach Bible classes and Brent sings in the choir and has done performance singing for Stonebriar Community Church where Chuck Swindoll is the pastor. Currently, Brent is President of the Northwestern University Alumni Association.

Angel finished Shell Lake High School as class valedictorian. She graduated from Northwestern College in Roseville, Minnesota. She was an MVP volleyball player and earned a degree in communications. She and her husband, Steve, are raising three children, two sons, and one daughter. The two oldest are in high school and the youngest in junior high. They have their home in Blaine, Minnesota.

Like all parents whose children grow up and leave home, we have to make the adjustment of embracing an empty nest. The story of our children honoring us with good marriages and strong Christian faith is a happy story, and we are extremely grateful to God to be able to give that report.

Chapter 12
The Scandalous Saint

I was never a big dreamer or goal setter in my life. I am, however, a kind of mover-shaker person. As a type A personality, my tendency is to push to get things done. I will admit that I'm not afraid to take some risks. I just call it stepping out in faith. I do believe when God gives you a good idea, you need to make decisions to move forward in faith and not just keep talking about ideas. I'm kind of a let's get started person. Usually, it took others to come alongside me to get things finished. Being a visionary makes it difficult to follow through to the finish because you always seem to get another vision and start pushing for that before the last one is complete.

That seems to be my life modus operandi (M.O.) It was never hard for me to believe God for big things nor to step into the waters. It can drive some people crazy to work with people like that while others love the challenge of taking risks. I will admit that those people who just want things to be status quo seem a bit boring to me. Okay, that's how God made me. I love adventure.

I love experiences. I could have fit right into the millennial generation very well. They love the challenge of extremes, adventure, and experiences. I must have been born with high-energy and an inquisitiveness to experience life. God has blessed my journey with many opportunities to meet incredible people, to see unimaginable places, and to do some exciting things. I could never have predicted, nor imagined what God had in store for my life when I committed my life to serve Him. He has done exceeding abundantly above all I could have ever thought or asked for.

Many of those experiences have resulted from our involvement with missionaries, mission fields, and with pastors who have opened their hearts for us to share ministry with their churches.

I mentioned in a previous chapter about my relationship with Pastor John Bell from San Antonio, Texas. Pastor Bell gave me my first opportunity to preach to his congregation when I was just starting our ministry. I was invited back several times over the years and spoke at their mission conferences several times. Pastor Bell was invited to be a guest speaker at our first world mission conference in Shell Lake in October of 1986. That has become an annual conference in October ever since. In October of 2016 will be our thirtieth annual World Missions Conference.

When John Bell passed away, his son David Bell took over the church in San Antonio, and they renamed it Destiny Church. David was the pastor for about fifteen years until he passed away suddenly while in his office on a Sunday morning before their service in 2011. I was privileged to have been invited on several occasions by David Bell to preach at Destiny Church. When David passed away at age fifty-seven, I was asked to preside over his burial service at the cemetery in San Antonio.

The successor to the pastorate of Destiny Church is Matthew Bell who is David's oldest son. Now the church entered into the third generation of the Bell family. Matthew has been very open with embracing our relationship and I have had the privilege to speak for him at Destiny Church. That makes three generations of the Bell family that I have preached for at Destiny Church in San Antonio.

Matthew Bell's heart has been enlarged to support world missions, which carries on his grandfather's legacy. John Bell was a missionary statesman and sent out scores of missionaries in his lifetime.

This October of 2016 is our thirtieth World Missions Conference. One of our conference speakers for this conference will be Matthew Bell, John Bell's grandson and pastor of Destiny Church. I will always be grateful for the relationship God has given us with the Bell family.

Missions have afforded me so many opportunities to travel to unimaginable places that I would never have dreamed to go.

My very first mission trip was to Mexico in the early 1970s to visit the work of missionary John Eils. A group of young singles loaded up in the church van and hooked up the Jeep to head to Mexico. Chuck Zosel came along to help me drive. One of the single ladies along with us was Debbie Durand. She was invited by her boyfriend's sister and didn't have any idea what kind of group and trip she was in for.

When we got to San Antonio, we stopped to stay overnight before traveling to Mexico the next day. I received a call that evening from Pastor John Bell who told me that he had scheduled a revival meeting from Sunday through Wednesday, but his scheduled speaker had gotten ill and would not be able to come for the meetings. I was shocked when he asked me to fill the pulpit in place of the other speaker. I wanted to back out of the offer because I was fearful that it was too big of an assignment for a young preacher from the little town of Shell Lake.

The group with us considered it a good opportunity for me, and they were excited for me and prayed right there that I would accept. It would be my first time to ever preach in a large city church.

I did agree to preach on Sunday morning and evening and can honestly say that I don't know what I said or how I did, but the group of twelve who were with me kept encouraging me by saying that it had gone well. We planned to leave for Mexico the next morning. Late Sunday evening, Pastor Bell contacted me again and told me that the main speaker still would not make it for Monday night service and asked if I could stay for one more night to preach. My thought was if I had not done well enough on Sunday, he wouldn't have asked me back for Monday night.

I will always thank the Lord for that opportunity to stay one more night. I closed the service with an invitation to come to the altar and receive Christ's salvation and forgiveness. I don't remember anyone who might have come except one. That was the night that Debbie Durand was wonderfully saved. She was the one person in our traveling group who had never known the Lord. This added a great deal of excitement to the rest of our trip.

Debbie married her boyfriend Roy Slater Jr. who later came to Christ and was called to the ministry. Years later there was a failure in their marriage and ministry, and they were divorced. Through time and a healing process, Debbie was married to Ron Huebner, and they both currently serve the Lord and are active members of Shell Lake Full Gospel Church.

Our trip into Mexico opened my eyes for the first time to what a real mission field looked like. John Eils took us to the villages and ranches where everyone was able to share their testimonies. That trip was the door that opened up for me what would become many doors of opportunities to become personally involved and to get the church involved with partnering with missionaries and nations around the world.

John Eils became a close friend of the church and a dear personal friend of Linda and I. He would fly his airplane on occasion to Shell Lake just to spend a few days with us. He loved Shell Lake.

One of our trips to Mexico, I traveled with Frank Holmes from Siren, Wisconsin. Frank was a native American evangelist who traveled into Canada and the U.S. and often would preach in some of the hardest regions of both nations where it was difficult for the gospel to penetrate. He was highly respected for his work among the native Indian people.

John Eils took Frank and me to a village in Mexico called La Pesca. We found there a family who John had previously ministered to. A man in the family, who was a husband and father of several children, was crippled and lying in bed. He had been lying in that bed for seventeen years unable to walk because of the curse of a witch doctor from that village. An old bag of herbs hung on a twine above the bed, and the witch doctor had pronounced a death sentence over him if he ever left his bed. John Eils had led this family to Christ but had not had success in praying for the man's healing. Frank Holmes showed them from the scripture how they could break that curse upon his life. He told them if the man would be willing to let us carry him out of the house and take the bag of herbs and let us burn it, God would bring change to them. Frank had done this many times among the natives he ministered to because of much superstition and witchcraft. We showed them the scripture from Acts 19:19, where the people brought their books on magic and witchcraft and burned them in the authority of the Name of the Lord Jesus.

John worked very hard to convince them that God would not let the man die if he would trust the Lord. I remember that the man finally permitted us to burn the bag of curses that had hung over his bed and held him captive for seventeen years. We did not bring the man outside, but we did light a fire and burn the bag. We prayed over the family and left.

I received a letter from John Eils six weeks later which stated that the man in the village of La Pesca had started learning to walk. After he was completely healed, the family donated the property next to their house for John Eils to build a church. The church is operating today in that fishing village.

John Eils was a maverick missionary who went to Mexico on his wedding night in Texas without any money to start a mission work. He and his wife Josie completely trusted God in the most unconventional ways. God made provisions that kept them there until John's untimely death in 1979. The story of my friend's life is best captured in a book about him written by the well-known pastor John Hagee from San Antonio, Texas. The book is called *The Scandalous Saint*. John Eils was a most unusual kind of missionary who had the deepest heart of love and compassion for the Hispanic people.

In 1979, John was taking three businessmen from Dallas, Texas in a small four-seat Cessna owned by one of the men to visit the church he had started in the village of La Pesca in Mexico. The plane was not piloted by John Eils. They were trying to make it to the village before the evening fog settled in from the coast. By the time they arrived, the fog was coming in and when the pilot found a small opening where could see around, they turned into a hillside and crashed. Only one of the men was thrown out of the plane and survived. John Eils and the other two men were unable to get out, and their bodies were burned.

My wife called me where I was a guest speaker in Belleville, Illinois. It was Sunday morning before service when she told me of John's death. It was heartbreaking for both of us to lose our dear friend. I flew from Belleview to San Antonio to attend John Eils' funeral. Pastor Bell and I had a brief meeting with John Hagee in his home to discuss with him what would happen to the orphanage in Mexico that John Eils had started in Ciudad, Victoria. A young lady named Jane Anderson (from our church in Shell Lake) was managing the orphanage when John was killed. I served on the board of the orphanage with John Hagee and wanted to know what he thought would happen to the orphanage. I was concerned for Jane's well-being.

Jane stayed on to manage the orphanage and a man by the name of Ralph Baker came down from the states to became the director of the orphanage. Only a few months after he arrived, Jane got a telephone call asking her to come to the mortuary in Ciudad Victoria (Mexico) to identify a man whose vehicle had been hit by a train on the way to the city. Jane identified him as Ralph Baker. A second director of the orphanage had been killed during Jane's time there. It was too much for Jane to handle so she came back home. The orphanage was taken over by John Hagee and is no longer operating.

This was a painful ending for our first exposure to the mission field and to the missionary we loved.

Chapter 13
Missions Adventures

I had several opportunities to travel with Evangelist Frank Holmes both in Mexico and Canada. Frank often ministered to the First Nations people.

On one trip I traveled with him in the month of January. I knew it would be a risk since Manitoba was known for high winds and snow. We were ministering at the Mallard Reservation. A cold front had come in with very high winds. The combined temperature with wind chill was listed at one hundred degrees below zero. At the home where we stayed, I noticed frost on the inside of the kitchen windows that was almost an inch thick.

Frank's car would not start so the natives kept a wood fire going under the motor block with a tarp over the hood. They kept the fire going for three days and nights before the oil was thin enough to get the car started.

On our way to minister at the next reservation which was about sixty miles away, a snow storm came. Frank's defrost was not working so he had to drive while looking through a small clearing in his windshield just above the dashboard. The winds came up, and the snow blinded us, making it impossible to see the road. A snow plow came along and almost hit us. Frank reacted by driving into the ditch. I nervously laughed at our continuing misfortunes. Frank soberly reminded me that this situation was no laughing matter. The car was being quickly buried under snow, and if God didn't help us, we could die there.

I quickly got serious, and we began to pray asking the Lord to help us get out of our fix. Frank asked me to run quickly to stand in the road if we saw headlights of any coming vehicle. I just couldn't believe that anybody else would be out driving in that blinding snow storm.

It wasn't until about thirty minutes later that I did see some headlights. I jumped from the car and stepped on the road waving for the vehicle to stop. When the driver saw me, he stopped and approached me with anger and cursing. I could tell he had been drinking so I apologized and gently asked for his help. He told me that the only reason he even stopped was because he remembered that his brother had been killed in an accident exactly one year before on that exact same day. Even though he would be late getting home, he offered to help us as a tribute to his brother. His brother had died only a half-mile up the road from where our vehicle was stranded.

He took us to town and got a chain. He then came back and pulled us out. We were finally able to drive on through the storm to the next reservation. God answered our prayers in a miraculous way. The man probably knew he had saved our lives. I might have thought he was an angel, except I don't think angels curse and swear.

On another trip to Canada with Frank, we took two other men with us. Roy Slater Jr. before he moved to Florida and Don Meyerson, a young minister from Minneapolis. Don never shrunk back from an adventure and is a servant leader who loves helping others. He was good to have along with us. We were headed to Oxford House Reserve in northern Manitoba. It was during late September, and the weather was cool.

On our way, we stopped to stay overnight in Cross Lake, Manitoba. Don stayed in my room, and Roy and Frank stayed in a house next door. When I woke up, Don was gone, and I heard some loud coughing and choking coming from next door. I went to see what was going on and saw smoke coming out the front door of the house where Roy and Frank were staying. Don had gotten up early to do a good service for the guys by lighting a fire in the kitchen stove. He had put some wood in the stove and put some papers on it and lit a fire. Don had not ever seen a stove like that and didn't realize that there was no smoke stack on the stove so the fire he had started to warm the house was started in the oven. His good deed was met with a smoking house and a couple of choking preachers. I was the only one who was laughing and good-naturedly called Don our city slicker.

Romania

In 2007, I traveled into Romania and across Moldova and Transnistria with evangelist Ghorghi Cazacu, whom we helped support for many years. Roy Peterson also traveled with us and developed a serious pain in his leg. It was cramping, and the pain was nearly unbearable.

We went to a Russian speaking church to sit in on their midweek prayer meeting which about a hundred people were attending. In that service, there was a woman who stood up and spoke a word of knowledge to the taller American. She was referring to Roy. she said that she saw the devil attacking his leg and that Roy was to take authority over that spirit to ease the pain. This she spoke in Russian which was interpreted into Romanian and then into English so we could understand. That woman had never seen Roy before nor did she know about his condition.

We returned to our hotel and went to bed. Roy woke up about 1:00 a.m. with intense pain and then remembered the words of that woman who told them to take authority over the devil. Roy did that and found immediate relief from the pain. God was faithful to help him through the gift of the Holy Spirit operating in a faithful Russian saint.

Mongolia

My trip to Mongolia with Russ Frase in 2012 to speak at a conference of three hundred first generation believers was another delightful opportunity. It was held in the city of Ulaanbaatar, the capital city.

We met with a woman who attended the conference. She was known as the foremost lawyer in the country of Mongolia. She wanted to meet with us privately to pray for her. The communist party knew her well and had threatened her for embracing the Christian faith. We prayed over her in our vehicle and told her where we were going to eat dinner. While we were sitting down to eat that evening, she walked in dressed entirely incognito. She did not look like the same woman who was dressed in western style earlier that day. I did not recognize her until she came over to sit down with us. Her purpose for coming was to ask us to pray for her to receive the baptism in the Holy Spirit. We prayed for her, and God moved in a precious way upon her.

Peru Missionaries

John Mortimer Sr. has been a missionary for over forty-five years with his wife, Helena. They served in Mexico for ten years and have served over thirty-five years on the Amazon River in Peru. They live on the Amazon River in Iquitos, Peru. John and I have been friends since we both came to the Lord in our late teens. They have claimed me as their pastor for most of their years in Peru. The story of their travels and missionary works is one that needs to be told by them because my words would not begin to adequately describe the challenges and successes of their life's work. We consider them our closest missionary friends. We honor them and the Lord for their sacrifice and commitment for giving their lives to bring Jesus to the Spanish-speaking peoples.

My travels to the Amazon have all been eventful. The heat and humidity are almost intolerable. Much of the Mortimer's work on the Amazon has been planting new churches and training national ministers. They have traveled hundreds of miles upriver to search for tribes that have never heard the name of Jesus. God has blessed them at times with various modes of transportation that include a Catamaran houseboat, outboard motor boats, airboats, a hovercraft, and large jet skis. What were previously three-day canoe trips up the river to reach remote villages has been cut down considerably with the faster modes of transportation.

On one of my trips to Peru, I brought along my friend John Slater from Turtle Lake, Wisconsin. John had married a lady who attended our church and owned a fishing lodge in Ontario, Canada. John and I flew to Iquitos to join the Mortimers on a river trip to visit some village churches. We traveled in a sixteen-foot aluminum boat with a 50 HP outboard motor. John (Fred) Mortimer, his wife Helen, John Slater, and I stayed in the villages for a few days.

The first village we came to was met with a near disaster. We parked at a dock on the river and spent some time visiting with the pastor and wife in their stilt home. The homes along the Amazon were built on stilts to survive the times of high water. After they had given us something to eat, we planned to move on to the next village. John Mortimer had been trying to start the motor which wouldn't start. He had pulled the spark plug to clean it and to check for spark. Helena and John Slater were already in the boat. I was standing on the dock ready to get in. At the back of the boat was a 50-gallon plastic container full of gasoline which we were bringing upriver. John Mortimer had some gasoline on his hands while working on the engine and was checking for spark on the plug. When he pulled the starter cord, the plug connection sparked and started an immediate fire on John's hands which spread to the gasoline that had leaked onto the barrel. Flames were everywhere, and John Mortimer leaped into the river to douse the flames on himself. He came up splashing water into the boat and onto the gasoline barrel. John Slater threw Helena onto the shore, and we all waited for the explosion. The explosion never happened. Fortunately, John Mortimer had filled the gasoline barrel to the cap. That meant there were no vapors in the barrel to cause it to explode. We were protected from a disaster. John did have second-degree burns on both hands, but he knew we had avoided a serious incident. We were all praising God for his care over us.

One-fifth of the world's river water lies within the borders of the Amazon River. In places, it is over four hundred feet deep. The mouth of the Amazon is ninety miles wide. It runs into the ocean with fresh water that extends up to two hundred fifty miles into the sea. The river is moving at seven miles per hour with large whirlpools swirling all over the river.

We had made one boat trip on the river in total darkness going back to Iquitos from preaching in one of the villages. Johnny Mortimer Jr. was driving the boat. He was guided by the light from his GPS (global positioning system). It shone bright enough that we could spot any debris above the water. Once we were traveling at nearly full speed when we hit a large log that was under water. It shook the boat, and really shook me. Johnny always drives with the transit on the motor unlocked, so the motor tilted up rather than ripping the stern off the back of the boat. I had more than one nightmare about trying to swim the turbulent Amazon in the middle of a black night.

God has blessed the Mortimer family as they have touched thousands of lives on the Amazon and reached unreached villages with the gospel. The legacy of John Mortimer's ministry has been passed on to his son Johnny and grandson Vince Mortimer.

Their journey to Peru began in Duluth, Minnesota in 1983. The Mortimers left Duluth for Iquitos, Peru starting on Lake Superior in a fifty-seven-foot Catamaran houseboat. They had purchased the boat in Knife River, Minnesota and it had already been named by the previous owner Crusader for Christ. God had shown that very boat in a dream to John several years before. Several of our Shell Lake church members stood on the shore of Lake Superior to say our goodbyes as the Mortimers left the port. We had all prayed over them. The entire trip by water from Duluth to Iquitos, Peru took a total of five years. It is a most incredible story of their journey and a miraculous one all along the way. Our relationship with all the Mortimer family remains very close.

Evangelist Frank Holmes and John and Helena Mortimer have been part of our church family as members of Full Gospel Church. They are also part of our heritage and renown as a small town congregation that has touched the world with the gospel of Jesus Christ.

Chapter 14
India — Mother Teresa

In 1993, I felt the Lord impressing upon me that I would be going to the country of India to encourage Julius Morar in the work he was doing there. I also planned to visit Julius' brother Sheal Morar.

Linda and I had met the parents of these two young men when they visited the states in the mid-nineteen seventies. Their father and mother were Mr. and Mrs. James Morar. The history of the ministry of the Morars goes back to the very early nineteen hundreds when a woman missionary by the name of Mrs. McCarty from the states led James Morar's father to Christ and baptized him.

Linda and I had housed the elder James Morar and his wife in our home on a couple occasions. They were highly principled people. It was through them that we became connected with their three sons, David, Sheal, and Julius. They are third generation ministers in India.

It was in 1995 that God made it possible for me to travel to India. I joined up with two other minister friends. David Bentley from Little Rock, Arkansas and David

Cerar who is now a missionary Bible teacher in Kenya, Africa. David Bentley was formerly a police inspector in Little Rock. He had a gift of faith for healings and became a prominent minister after his police retirement. I deeply respect his man.

The three of us were met in Calcutta by Julius and his wife, Ruth. We traveled another twenty-two hours by train to the city of Gorakhpur where Julius had started a church, a Christian school for very poor children, and a Bible college. Julius asked if we would dedicate the Christian school which had thirty-eight children attending. We also dedicated the new Bible school that was built on the second story of his home.

David Bentley was led by the Lord to begin a feeding program in the Christian school where he promised to feed each student one meal each school day. The children were so poor that most of them were able to get just a small portion of food at their homes once a day. We could see how malnourished they were.

David has kept that promise since 1995, and even when the school attendance increased to nearly 800 students, David has found a way to raise support to continue feeding one meal a day to every student. One of David's sons has continued with the feeding program. God had chosen David to come with me through an unusual circumstance.

A few weeks before leaving for India, I had called David Bentley to ask if he could come with me. He told me that he was going to go to Pakistan at the same time and could not travel with me. So it would be David Cerar and me who would travel together.

I received a call from David Bentley two weeks before our flight, and he told me that the trip to Pakistan had fallen through and that he would go with us to India if we still wanted him to come. We worked everything out to travel together and found that it was no secret why God had purposed for David Bentley to travel with us.

Our dear friends, the Morars, gave us several opportunities to minister in several churches in the northern part of India and into the country of Nepal. It was refreshing to see the deep hunger in the hearts of the people to know Christ as Lord and Savior and to receive His Holy Spirit. David Bentley helped us with our faith to pray for and see people healed and received miracles. We prayed with so many Muslim and Hindu people to receive Jesus as Savior.

Our trip into Nepal was very special. The nation had only been free from communist oppression since 1990. The people were so hungry for the light and truth about Jesus and the gospel. At one church where I spoke, the people were just beginning to adjust to their liberty of worshipping the Lord freely. There were still some fears from years of oppression and persecution. We knew we had to pray that the curses based on fear would be broken. God broke through, and tears flowed down the cheeks from men and women who knew they had been set free by the loving authority of Christ.

I remember at the close of one service, we were in prayer to dismiss when a family of two adults and three children came into the church. The pastor told Julius that these people had heard about the service with the Americans and had walked through the mountains for three days to come to the service. They made it only in time for the closing prayer. I felt humbled by their efforts and asked if we could stay for a while and personally minister and pray for them. I think we all wept a little as we saw their hunger and interest in hearing about Jesus. They received all that we could give them, and then left to walk another three days home.

I must say that short-term mission trips have had a life-changing effect on my worldview and one of the reasons why we have been so active to maintain our focus on missions.

We went to Calcutta to prepare for our flight back to the states. We had one day to spend in this diverse city of millions of people, thousands of sacred cows in the streets, and myriads of slums and shanties that housed the poorest and lowest caste people of India. Thirty-three percent of households live in slums without any basic services provided by the municipality. But the city also is known for its cultural art and literature. There were many high and low rise buildings and well-maintained science centers and theaters. On one street there was a half-mile of bookshops and bookstalls spilling over onto the pavement.

The human rickshaws (taxis with humans pulling carts) were all over. David Cerar and I did take a ride in one. I felt like I was violating human rights so I gave the man a tip that would equal his week's wage.

We had a few hours left to spend in the afternoon in Calcutta before heading to the airport for our flight home. Our chauffeur was Julius Morar's father-in-law. I asked if he thought we could visit Mother Teresa at her residence. He said that we could try. When I knocked at her door, I was told by a caretaker that she was sleeping. I told her that we would come back later.

I had heard for many years about an American missionary who had come to India in 1954 to minister love and compassion of Christ to the destitute on the streets of Calcutta. He had stayed his entire life helping these people and building up a large church in the city. His reputation for the work he has done in Calcutta is known by the people in the city equally to that of Mother Teresa. His name is Mark Buntain. During Mark Buntain's fifty years of ministry in Calcutta, the ministry has grown to include 800 churches, several Bible colleges, a hospital, and a teacher's college. Mark passed away in 1989.

David Cerar and I spent a little time visiting the grave of Mark Buntain which was located at the Memorial Church that he pastored.

We returned to Mother Teresa's resident and were permitted to enter. I was escorted to a balcony that was divided by a curtain to her living quarters. I realized that this was a historic moment about to happen for me, and I wondered what I was going to say.

When Mother Teresa walked through the curtain she extended her hands to me and said, "Welcome my son, what can I do for you? Have you come to help my people?" I told her that I had and that my heart was compassionate for them. I then commented that she had given a wonderful speech at the Washington prayer breakfast during the time when Bill Clinton was president and Al Gore was Vice President.

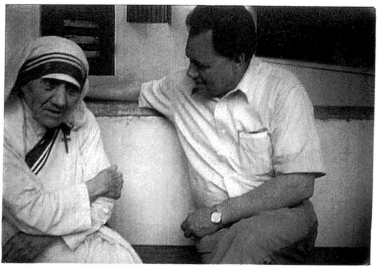

Pastor Amundson with Mother Teresa.

She had said in her speech that the United States kills too many babies. She told the president to let the children be born, and if they were not wanted, she would take them. She told them that the greatest threat to world peace is abortion.

She seemed to be pleased with my comment and asked me if I would like her manuscript of the speech. I have kept that manuscript and a picture of her sitting on a crudely made bench holding my hands. We had a thirty-minute conversation of which I can recall almost every word. She told me that "for love to be real, it must cost something—it must empty us of self." I blessed her in the name of Jesus as we left.

We visited the center for the dying that she had started. Every day there are people who are near death that are found in the streets of the city. Mother Teresa believed that all of her people should be able to die with dignity.

When we entered the center for the dying, we saw about seventy-five men and women being scrubbed and cleaned and new clothes being put on them. There were volunteers from around the world who donated six months of their lives to care for the diseased and dying people who were taken off the streets. The images of the people I saw was a rebuke to my complacency toward the needs of the suffering and unloved.

Julius Morar is incredibly intelligent. Like many gifted, native Indians, he has used his gifts and resources to provide a better life for many of his people. I'm honored to be called one of his spiritual fathers. He and his wife Ruth and son Jonathan currently reside in Riverside, California. He continues to maintain all of his ministries in Gorakhpur, India.

Chapter 15
Marching to Pretoria

It was 2004, during the October Missions Conference in Shell Lake that we met a couple from Pretoria, South Africa. They had been invited to come to the conference as guests for the first time. Their names are Ron and Rina Kinnear.

Ron has helped to establish Bible training schools in several African countries. He helps to educate young African refugees from civil war-torn nations in Africa and train them for ministry.

Rina is an intercessor for Africa and has established herself as a spiritual leader and speaker at women's conferences in South Africa.

Neither Ron nor Rina had come to our mission conference with any expectations except to build relationships with other missionaries and pastors who were in attendance. God had other plans in mind for them.

During the conference, I introduced them to the assembly. I asked them to share a brief report on their work in Africa. Ron mentioned that he was building and finishing a new Bible school just outside the city of Pretoria. They were struggling to purchase the electrical plant needed for power to run the school. Ron stated the cost was about seventeen thousand dollars.

One of the missionaries in the service walked to the platform and placed a hundred-dollar bill there. Several other missionaries placed money on the platform. Other people in the service began to place money on the platform until money was laying everywhere.

When it was all done, the ushers picked up the money to count it. When they came back with the report, the total reached over seventeen thousand dollars. The lights would be able to come on at the Pretoria Bible School.

In 2005, Paul Avery, David Lusse, and I flew to London, England to spend three days with Kelton Black who pastored a church in Highbridge, Somerset, England. I ministered in his church on Sunday, and Kelton gave us a tour of some historical places in the Somerset region. He took us to see the cleft in the rock from which Rev. A.M. Toplady wrote the hymn "Rock of Ages, cleft for me, let me hide myself in thee." This was written in 1762 after finding shelter in the cleft during a storm.

We were given a one-day tour of London and then boarded our plane to fly to Johannesburg, South Africa.

The Kinnears met the three of us and we stayed in their home in Pretoria for several days. It didn't take long for us to discover another power source that drives the success to the Kinnear's ministry. Each morning at

5:30 a.m. we could hear Rina Kinnear praying with loud intercession from her prayer chamber. She prays over an hour each morning before she starts her day and then prepares breakfast for her guests.

One of our purposes for traveling to Pretoria was to dedicate the Bible college and to turn on the electricity from the power plant that had been purchased from the funds that were raised at the Shell Lake Missions Conference.

It was a heartwarming movement to see the "thank you Shell Lake" signs that were posted on the walls outside of the office building. We felt the Holy Spirit's presence as we prayed the dedication prayer over the school followed by putting my hand on the switch and turning the power on.

Paul, David, and I traveled with the Kinnears to Mozambique where we did ministry. David Lusse and I became friends shortly after he and his wife Eilene moved to Poynette, Wisconsin from South Africa. Eilene had received a computer job in Madison to help prevent computer problems that the nation feared might happen during the Y2K phobia at the turn of the century.

David was raised in Namibia, Africa and worked with the Conservation Department until God released him to minister the gospel in several African countries. I met him at our missions conference which he had heard about from Ted Manning who attended a church in Madison. I loved having David with me on two of our trips to Africa. David loved African wildlife and had hunted many exotic game animals. He thrilled me with his stories about elephants and lionesses that circled his pickup truck in the night while he tried to sleep in his truck bed. His job was to do special surveys of wildlife health for the animal health department.

The Kinnears took us on a tour through Kruger National Park where we saw all the African animals in their natural environment. We drove close to the animals, and it was like being on a safari. David gave us his professional insights and stories about many of the animals.

David, Paul, and I were guests of Ron and Christi Bishop for several days in Botswana, Africa. Ron was caring for the ministry of Love Botswana which was a compound with a school and church that was started by Jerry Lackey and his wife. Jerry had returned to the states to raise funds for the operations expense and had planned to stay in the states for one year. Ron and Christi were left in charge of the ministry.

I remember the Sunday morning I was to preach in a tent that was packed with over three hundred people. I had developed laryngitis, and my voice had completely left me. I knew that without God's healing that I would not be able to preach. I was sure God would come through but the time was near for me to speak and I still had no voice whatsoever.

An American couple who were working at the compound were in the service. The woman was an accomplished singer. Just before my time to speak, she got up to sing. The song she sang with an incredibly beautiful voice was, "It is well with my soul." God's spirit swept over me, and I began to weep. I wept through the entire song. As soon as the song was over, Ron called me to come. Until the moment I opened my mouth, I had no voice. At first, I sounded squeaky but in a couple minutes, my voice was strong enough to be heard in the back of the tent. At the end of the message, I invited those who needed Christ as their Lord and Savior to come to the altar. I had assumed they probably were all Christians but rejoiced to see eighteen adults come to the altar to repent and give their hearts and lives to Jesus. Many were weeping, including me, in my amazement of God's goodness and grace to help me.

The day we were to leave Botswana, Ron Bishop took us to the airport to meet the Lackeys who had flown back from the states six months early. We met them at the airport, and we joined them for breakfast together. Ron had told us earlier that the Lackeys couldn't stay any longer in the states to raise funds. They were heartbroken to leave Botswana where they had lived most of their adult lives. They had originally been sent to Botswana with full financial support from Pastor John Osteen in Houston, Texas. Their entire compound and school had been financed by Pastor Osteen's ministry. The Lackeys had never had to try to raise more support for their ministry and felt very uncomfortable and lost while in the states. They had battled sickness and discouragement almost the whole time, so they came back early.

At breakfast, we were told by the Lackeys that when Pastor Osteen died, his son Joel took over the ministry.

When Joel bought the basketball complex in Houston, he made the decision to stop supporting some of his father's missionaries. The Lackeys and "Love Botswana" ministries were included in that decision. Ron and Christi returned to the states and are currently residing for a time in Ireland where they continue to fill pulpits and teach. They have remained our dear friends for over forty years and are the most well-traveled Bible teachers I know, having ministered in over seventy countries.

Africa, known as the dark continent, is brighter today because of the spreading of the gospel. It is brighter because missionaries have carried the torch of the message of Jesus, the light of the world. It is brighter because a small town church in Shell Lake, Wisconsin has helped raise up millions of dollars to support those missionaries who carry the torch. We are a church that unselfishly has not sought our own welfare, but the welfare of others and God has returned the blessings far more than we feel we deserve.

Chapter 16
Local Church Missions

Missions starts with a world view. We must feel God's heart for the world. It was the world that God so loved!

During our first year of ministry in Shell Lake, I put out a challenge to our few people attending the church. We set a goal to give $1,000 to missions. There was some resistance to that challenge, so I told them that if our general church budget dropped because of our mission giving that we would discontinue giving to missions.

At the end of our fiscal year, we had given more than the $1,000 and the general budget of the church had also increased. We increased our second year to $3,000, and the general budget had increased as well. We were on our way to becoming a missionary church.

In 1986, we held our first missionary conference in Shell Lake. We formed a missions committee to help prepare housing for the missionaries who attended the conference.

Arvid Moin was on our staff and came up with the idea of how to help our people make personal connections to the missionaries. He asked for members to open their homes to house a missionary four nights during the conference. Those who couldn't provide their home could choose to provide an evening meal for a missionary during the conference.

Our people were willing to respond, and that began thirty years of providing housing and meals by church members for conference attendees during every annual missions conference. The idea has worked well to connect our people with the missionaries through the years.

The missionaries have been trusted not to solicit support from the people they become acquainted with in the congregation. We have had very few problems.

The number of member missionaries has grown every year as their applications are approved. We are still keeping up with the housing needs and the church now provides most meals for guest missionaries and ministers.

What started with just over $10,000 given to missions in our first conference in 1986 has grown where we now help support over sixty missionaries in thirty-seven countries of the world. In 2010 Full Gospel Church was able to give $499,000 to missions. Of course, there are others who now help our mission budget from outside of the church. They see the value of what we are doing and are partnering with us. Money now comes in from other supporters.

Also included in support of our missions budget is a tithe to missions from our church budget. The idea to tithe from the church tithes and offerings came at a time when our church budget was not growing. We were struggling to meet payroll and keep the church bills paid.

Our church treasurer during that period was Candie Peterson. Her husband Roy was serving as an elder in the church. Roy and Candie were praying and asking God for a financial breakthrough. One night the Lord put a thought into their hearts. They met with myself and the elders and proposed that if the church would begin to tithe from its own budget, God would pour out greater blessings upon the church finances.

At our lowest point financially, we took a leap of faith and sowed the church's firstfruits into missions. We increased monthly support to our member missionaries. We also set up an emergency account to help fund urgent needs. This account is still in place.

The first thing we noticed during the next few months after we began tithing into missions was an increase in church giving. The church budget grew, and all the needs were met. God had blessed our church finances. We have never stopped tithing into missions.

My friend Pastor John Bell was a missionary states-man. He and his wife Ruth had served in Japan as missionaries before they were pastors in San Antonio, Texas. John understood missions and his church was a fore-runner and model for our church in conducting mission conferences. He was our first conference speaker when we started in 1986.

I heard Pastor Bell say more than once that when-ever he would notice his own church budget getting low in funds, he would say that was the time for the church to take up a missionary offering. For some reason, a blessing would come upon the church finances afterward. I believe that is because missions is the heartbeat of God. The Great Commission is to take the gospel to the world. Our church has also discovered that whenever we get into a tight spot financially, the best thing we can do is to give to some missions project. It brings a spirit of faith and expectancy, and the needs of our own church finances are met.

I believe that generations to come will dictate the course of nations for Christ. It will be because we are willing to live unselfishly to accomplish what must be done for others to receive the gospel.

Often during our missions conference, we will see missionaries sow their own funds into the support of other missionaries to help them with their projects. Missionaries are such giving people, and the ones who I know do not give their funds in hopes that they will wow people to give back to them. They give because they know what the needs feel like on the other end. They know that God takes care of their needs.

In one conference, we had a guest come who was not a member of the conference. His name was Jeff Rogers, who along with his wife had served as missionaries for several years. She was born and raised in Zimbabwe. Jeff was raised in Texas.

Jeff and his wife had developed a school for children's education and nearly two thousand students. They had established a church in Zimbabwe, and were helping AIDS victims, and were feeding the school children one meal a day. God had provided the funds to develop their work.

President Robert Mugabe was a dictator who held tight control over the people. He ruled by terror and was euthanizing the people by cutting off water supplies in the cities and cutting off food supplies. Jeff told me that at that time there were over five million lives that had been destroyed.

Jeff had made the decision to leave Zimbabwe and go to Washington D.C. to lobby our government to place sanctions on Mugabe. The word got back to Zimbabwe and Mugabe placed a price on the head of Jeff Rogers, wanting him dead. Jeff never returned to Zimbabwe.

While I was visiting Jeff in a restaurant and as he was telling me his story, he received a call from a lady in Zimbabwe who he had left in charge of the school. She was crying, and I noticed tears running down the cheeks of Jeff as he was talking. After he had hung up, I was told what the call was about. The woman said that the water supply had been cut off, and there was no clean water.

They had been purifying ground water by boiling it and had run out of wood. She was having to destroy the furniture that was available to use for a fire. She said the rice and millet they were using for food was running out.

Jeff had made arrangements in Johannesburg, South Africa to buy thirty tons of millet which was ready to be shipped. He had a source to get it across the border to the school, but he did not have the funds to ship it to the border. I asked him how much it would cost to ship it, and he told me fifteen thousand dollars. I checked out some sources who verified that the school was built by Jeff and the needs were acute ones.

I asked Jeff to address the conference for a few minutes and tell the story. I asked the people if anyone wanted to help ship the millet from South Africa. The response was immediate. When the offering was received and counted, and the report was over twenty thousand dollars came in to ship the millet to the border of Zimbabwe. Jeff saw to it that the millet was brought across the border in few cases at a time.

Two years later when I saw Jeff he told me that there was still food in the warehouse and was getting near the end. The woman in charge of the school told him that even though they used up the same amount every day, she noticed that the stock had stopped dwindling. She saw the same amount of millet in the storage even though she was continually taking it out. God had done something special to the gift we had given to feed the children. That miracle was started by one of the missionaries who was the first to deposit his offering upon the platform. It released the spirit of giving upon the conference that evening.

First fruit Giving

I think that there is an important word to be said about firstfruits. These are gifts that are given from the top. They are gifts that are given first. It always touches my heart to see missionaries often jump first into giving toward another missionary's needs.

Proverbs 3:9 tells us to "honor the Lord with ... the first fruits of all your increase" (NKJV). Firstfruits are simply an indicator of honoring God for his blessings and releasing back to him the very first of our blessings.

Our Shell Lake community used to have a radio station that sponsored Christian programming. I served on the committee that raised funds to sponsor the Christian programs. Volunteer donations kept the station going. Each year we would ask pastors from the area to come to the station to help raise funds for Christian programming. They would each take a couple hours to encourage people to send in gifts. Many of them would appeal to the listeners to send in monies to sponsor a favorite program. I noticed that most of them would ask for support from others but would make no contributions themselves. They were the hosts whom I noticed would receive the lowest responses.

The ones who received the most responses were those who first made their own commitment and sacrifices themselves, and then make a challenging appeal.

Through the years I have found that to make an appeal for funds to support any church project, it would work best if I sowed the first fruit offering and then ask the congregation to get on board. God blessed the best when we made the first sacrifice. First fruit giving and the blessing from it works for everyone.

Linda and I have always partnered with biblical giving of tithing our income to the church we worship in. When we began to see the heart of God in missions, we felt the need to give a second tithe of our income into missions. That has been our greatest joy.

Chapter 17
Cast Your Bread
Upon the Waters

Years ago I read the scripture from Ecclesiastes 11:1 "Cast your bread upon the waters, and you will find it after many days" (RSV). I really have read this verse many times, but it became real to me after seeing the results of our mission conferences.

China

During our missions conferences in the mid-1990's, I met a couple who attended and said that they were called to go to China. They were Mike and Lisa Haller from the small community of Gordon, Wisconsin. Mike had taken early retirement from the telephone company. Lisa grew up in Malaysia and met Mike while he was in the service. They married and have three lovely daughters.

I asked Mike when they were leaving to do missionary work in China. He told me they were waiting for the support to come in so they could live in China. They are a quiet couple, and it was difficult for them to mention their needs to me. They filled out an application for membership to our conference and attended each year for three years. Mike and Lisa were introduced to the conference each year and told the people that they were going to China.

The fourth year they attended, they still had not been able to go to China. Their home church would help to back them. They sat through the entire conference, once again standing before the people to tell them that God had called them to China. This time, they mentioned that they would need four hundred dollars more support each month before they could go.

At the close of the conference, I was dismissing in prayer and had just said the Amen to go home when a lady in the congregation raised her hand high and yelled out for me to listen to her.

Those who know Rita Siebens know that she can easily be heard when she wants to. I stopped everyone to listen to her. She said that God had just put in her heart the word ten dollars. She told us that if forty people would give ten dollars a month toward the Haller's need, they could go to China! In thirty seconds there were forty people who committed. The Hallers were ready and, in a few weeks, they left as a family for China and began working with orphaned boys with physical defects at an orphanage. The Hallers have served there faithfully for over twenty years. The church had cast our bread upon the waters in China.

The oldest daughter's name is Jill. She and her sisters were sitting in the back pew of the church on the night the final funds were raised for their parents to leave for China. The girls had been sitting in that last row each of the four years they attended the conference. Jill had grown into a teenager and her sisters not far behind. Waiting for the dream to come true for them at that age must have seemed like a long, long time.

I was able to see the expression on the girl's faces as they realized what had just happened. They really were going to China! All three of them were crying uncontrollably as the realization set in.

The Haller family did not come home very often, but the girls readily adapted to the Chinese culture. Jill, the oldest, married and she and her husband started a small business in Beijing.

It was fifteen years after the Hallers moved to China that we were preparing for our twenty-fourth annual World Missions Conference. One week before the conference a letter was brought into my office by my secretary. I opened it and read the note written to the church from Jill (Haller) Coyle. She reminded us of that service when the church raised the money to send her family to China. She was so impacted by our missions conference and so thrilled at what God had done in their lives that she enclosed a check from herself and her husband and the little business they had developed. The check was made out to Full Gospel Missions for fifteen thousand dollars!

We had cast our bread upon the waters, and it came back with butter on it to bless many more missionaries.

Haïti

The church began to cast our bread into Haiti in the early 1980's. In 1985 we made our first trips to Haiti with Rev. A.D. Van Hoose's son, Deon. It opened my eyes to the world of poverty and filth. I couldn't begin to imagine what could ever be done to relieve the conditions of such poor people. Haiti is the poorest country in the Western Hemisphere.

We made our first contact with a young man by the name of Yves Regaillard. As a child, Yves was offered as a sacrifice in a voodoo worship ritual. The evil worshipers had cut off his nose before his grandmother intervened and brought him to a hospital. Yves had no place or no one to go to so he lived in that hospital for five years. It was through the mercy and compassion of an American Christian family that Yves was brought to the U.S. He was adopted by a white family with three daughters. The family, along with Pastor Van Hoose's church in Evansville, Indiana provided medical help for Yves and his nose was reconstructed and health restored.

Yves graduated from high school and went to college and afterward returned back to Haiti to help serve his people.

Our church built a close relationship with Yves as he was starting schools for children's education and was helping pastors strengthen their churches.

In the early years, we would purchase fifty-pound rice bags and distributed smaller bags of rice to families in the churches. Rice is the main staple food, but it is also expensive, so it is hard for families to buy. We would try to be careful that the village people didn't get wind that we were bringing rice to the church people. With hunger everywhere, the people would fight and got out of control easily if they knew where they could get rice.

At one church in on the coast, we were bringing in rice. Sheldon Dwyer was with us. Sheldon has been a missionary in the Philippines for over forty years. He is a nephew to my pastor, C.L. Warner. He has taught in Bible schools and trained hundreds of ministers in the Philippines.

Somehow the people in the village had heard that we might have some rice. Our intentions were to give packages of rice to the church people after the service. We noticed villagers pressing their faces against the window bars from outside. They were yelling and reaching through the windows asking for some rice. The men outside were pushing against the iron bars of the main doors. There was panic inside from the people in the church who were afraid their rice would be stolen.

The gates of the doors broke down, and one of the gates toppled on top of Sheldon. He was on the floor under the gate with dozens of people on top of him. I was screaming for help to get him out, and the pastor and some men came along to get the people off of the gate. We got Sheldon out and looked around to see rice scattered all over the floor. The people were scooping it up with their hands and the women packing what they could get into their dresses. People were fighting to take it away from others. It was a sight that I won't forget. We

119

changed our method of distributing rice after that incident. Hungry people will do desperate things.

Roy and Candie Peterson have made several trips to Haiti. We started a clothing distribution in Haiti and would ship clothing from a collection point we had in Spooner. People dropped off clothing and volunteers would bundle them, and we would ship them in barrels. That plan eventually had to be canceled because too much of the clothing that we sent was being stolen and sold on the black market.

We had saved up some clothing in Haiti to deliver to the people. Roy, Candie, and I were in a pickup truck passing clothes out to the poorer areas where people had little clothes to wear. People came running up to us trying to grab anything we had to give. Our clothes disappeared so fast and after it was gone there were some ladies who came crying to us asking for some clothes. They had very little clothing on. When we didn't have anything left to give them, Candie started crying because we had nothing left to pass out. Because of such desperate needs in Haiti, most of those on our teams who have traveled with us find themselves crying at times because we are not able to do more to help the people.

Our youth director, Dan Slater, has a compassionate heart for missions. He works closely with Yves Regalliard in Haiti. Dan has taken several medical teams of doctors, nurses, and dentists to provide short-term medical and dental care. They will often care for six to eight hundred people during each trip.

In March 2016 Dan Slater, Jeff Leonard, and his son Jacob finished installing the electricity, lighting, and sound into the auditorium addition onto the school. The addition was 82 feet by 150 feet. It is used to conduct ministry conferences. I remember that it took fifteen years to complete the walls and roof of the auditorium.

Dr. Timothy Warner is president of Haiti Missions and presided over the dedication of the new facility in March 2016. Two thousand people attended, and it was a huge success.

We had seen the very beginning of the school that Yves had started. When Roy, Kleon Cronk, and I were in Haiti in 2001, the school was small and inadequate. With help from Full Gospel Church and Northern Lights Christian Center in Hayward, the school now has three stories, a new auditorium, three hundred students, and qualified teachers supported by Haiti Missions.

Haiti has been a reality check for many people in our congregation who have been part of the short-term trips we have taken through the years. It has especially been an eye opener for the younger generation that has never encountered hardship, poverty, or lack. To be exposed to the spiritual darkness of spiritism and voodoo that thrives in abject poverty reveals the reality of how evil these false beliefs are and the damage that comes with them. In many of my stays in Haiti, my sleep at night has been interrupted by the beat of voodoo drummers and the incessant chants of worshipers of the devil. I believe the biggest cause of poverty in Haiti is the curses that are brought over the country by the people themselves.

In 2007 a woman from Haiti visited our church on a Sunday morning. Her name was Denise, and she was in Shell Lake to visit a medical doctor who was one of the doctors that went to Haiti on one of our first medical trips. On the way back to Shell Lake, the doctor became acquainted somehow with Denise. They became friends and Denise came to visit Shell Lake and spend time with Dr. Margaret.

On the Sunday that Denise visited our church, she was surprised to hear me speak of our church involvement with Haiti. She felt comfortable in discovering that our congregation loved the people of Haiti. I was introduced to Denise after the service, and she told me her story.

Denise had been a civil court judge in Haiti and was of the Catholic faith. The principles of her faith prevented her from accepting bribes to allow criminals not to be sentenced for their crimes. Consequently, she was threatened and the life of her daughter Becky was also threatened. Denise was divorced from her husband who was a Haitian medical doctor. For fear of losing her daughter because of threats against her, Denise and Becky moved to Miami.

One of the ladies in the church, Sandi Beecroft, befriended Denise and took her and Becky into her home for a brief time. As this Haitian mother and daughter continued coming to the church, both of them turned to Christ and were saved and baptized in water.

Denise began to bring other family members from Haiti to Shell Lake. She brought her mother and father and several other relatives who came directly from Haiti or had been staying in Miami. They all began coming to our mostly white congregation in rural northwest Wisconsin. It was amazing to see every one of them surrender their hearts to Jesus and be baptized in water. God filled several of them with His baptism of the Holy Spirit. It was a very strange scenario for us.

We had sown the gospel, helped build a school, clothed and fed the people, preached in the churches, and trained national pastors for many years in Haiti.

We had cast our bread upon the waters of Haiti, now God had sent it back with jam on it by sending souls all the way from Haiti to Shell Lake to get saved. All of those people whom God had sent to us have gone on to further educate themselves. The judge, Denise, returned to Haiti to her job. Her ex-husband, Bethel, became my friend, and I baptized him. He is furthering his degree to become a doctor in the states. Denise's nephew, Dede, was trained for ministry in Rice Lake and now is a pastor in Haiti. Another nephew is in Minneapolis; he is also studying medicine.

God works in strange but marvelous ways. His word does not return void. In this case, He returned our bread back to us all buttered and with jam on it.

Chapter 18
A House in Kona

The Jesus Movement in the early 1970's had a huge impact on our region, and there were many young people who were saved and baptized in water. In the Spooner/ Shell Lake area, youth gathered at the Shell Lake beachfront to talk about Jesus and to listen to ballads and folk gospel music. Whoever had a guitar would draw a small crowd around them, and each group would be singing and sharing their faith. This was happening during the summer months. In the fall, when school started, we would hold youth gatherings in our home. They were led by Ted Slater who came to the Lord during that time. Ted would play his guitar, lead the worship, and pray with the young people. Our house was filled with kids from high school. Many of those kids had received a definite personal experience with the Holy Spirit.

One of the young men who got saved during the Jesus Movement was Tim Bauer from Spooner. I remember Tim helping me with the many water baptisms that we were doing in Shell Lake. He had a passion for the

Lord that would lead him to a lifetime of ministry into the nations around the world.

Tim married JoAnn Crosby from Shell Lake. She was raised on a farm west of town and has devoted herself to help her husband throughout their years of ministry in several nations of the world.

Tim and JoAnn joined Youth With A Mission (YWAM) and have served with that ministry for over thirty-five years. The greatest portion of their financial support is from their sending church, Cornerstone Church in Spooner, Wisconsin.

I remained friends with Tim and JoAnn all through the years they have served with YWAM. They joined the membership of our World Missions Conference at a time when they were struggling to meet the financial needs of their family and their ministry. Our missions conference was able to raise a considerable amount of support to help them.

Tim poured his life into learning languages and biblical studies to help with teaching and training students in other countries. The Bauers lived in France while learning French. They have since served on the Island of Réunion and in Cyprus, Mombasa, Kenya, Switzerland, Holland, Madagascar, Taiwan, and Hong Kong. Their current home base is Kona, Hawaii where the main YWAM base is located.

Tim also spent a few years in Tyler, Texas working with Mercy Ships as a personnel coordinator. They bought an old house and did some remodeling with help from some of the tradespeople in Spooner and Shell Lake who went to Tyler and assisted them. I remember Ed Chupp, from our congregation, helped them build new cabinets and cupboards. This helped Tim and JoAnn to build up equity in their home.

The Bauers lived in Tyler, Texas for nearly three years. God then opened a new door for them to move to Kona, Hawaii. They sold their home and along with their three children moved to the YWAM base in Kona. Tim served as a teacher there and trained teams of students to go into Asia to befriend other students and share the gospel of Christ with them.

I have always admired Tim's long-term commitment serving as a leader with the international ministry of YWAM. I consider him among the most notable missionaries in the twenty-first century. When he left the small town of Spooner with his wife JoAnn, they never looked back, they just obeyed the call to go to the nations.

On one of the Bauer's trips home to visit family, I called Tim to ask if we could meet together for breakfast. God had given me an idea to pass along to Tim. He agreed to meet. In our meeting, I proposed an idea for him to consider for his future. Tim shared with me that he never had funds to plan for the time when he might retire from the ministry. When they moved to Kona, Hawaii, they did have some profits from the sale of their house in Tyler, Texas. He decided to invest in a piece of property that someone had offered at a special price for him. It was a buildable lot in Kona with an ocean view.

My idea was to try to help Tim and JoAnn make plans to build a home of their own. We could ask the various trades people from both congregations in Spooner and Shell Lake to contribute their time and talent to help the Bauers build their house. Tim and JoAnn would provide the housing and food for those who would go to Hawaii.

We needed a general contractor from here who could work with a contractor from there. We passed this idea to Jeff Burch from Spooner. He was a respectable builder in the area and was a longtime friend to both of us.

Jeff knew the challenge would be to find enough guys who could take the time to invest in the project. He approached plumbers, electricians, framers, cement workers, sheetrock hangers and finishers, and others who agreed to help the Bauers.

Tim had enough equity to get a construction loan and with Jeff coordinating the workers from here, they were able to build the house in Kona for the Bauer family in less than a year.

The Bauers now have a beautiful home that can also serve them into their future retirement thanks to the generous cooperation of believers who offered their skills to invest in the lives of two special missionaries, Tim and JoAnn Bauer.

My greatest joy and pleasure in life comes from investing into the lives of other people. I love to see others grow to the place where they can be used by the Lord to bless others. I believe in delegating responsibility to others to give opportunities for them to become fruitful. The people who have come to me with their idea of what the church needs or what ministry we need to develop are met with the same response: "Do you believe that it's an idea from the Lord?" If they answered yes, I would tell them that they had the job of developing their idea.

I had been mentored and given responsibility by my pastor which helped me grow as a leader so I believed in doing the same with those who led our ministries in the church. The test of a true leader is whether they really have a heart to serve.

I have watched my successor, Reg Myers, demonstrate a heart to serve. He first volunteered to be the church janitor. He and his wife volunteered to do childcare for people attending Sunday evening services. He started and led a men's prayer group that meets every Tuesday morning at 6:30 a.m. that has continued for many years. Reg prepared his devotional life with regular fasting and early morning prayer. He never asked me for any position in the church. We could see that God had greater plans for Reg, and so we hired him on our staff as an associate pastor. At first, Reg served as the leader of our Compassion Ministry for restoring men with addictions. At the same time, he completed his Bachelor's and Master's Degrees in Biblical Studies. He was appointed as an elder in the church. He has now been chosen as the successor to my pastoral leadership as I step down from my role as senior pastor on October 31, 2016.

Two other members of the ministry team serving in pastoral leadership are Dan and Jennifer Slater. I have enjoyed mentoring them into their leadership roles in the church. They have the greatest hearts to serve the people and now have become spiritual parents and mentors to many others who have grown up under their ministries. We all have an eye for people within our congregation whom we can develop and grow into leadership and servant roles in the church.

The ministry of mentoring is our assurance of raising up leaders who have the DNA of our ministry and who are able to stay with the flow of ministry that God has established for His work in Shell Lake. I think there are some pastors who have difficulty in delegating and releasing others to do the work of ministry, I see this as the most effective way to do God's work, through multiplying God's workers.

One of the reasons why we do short-term mission trips is to ignite a passion for serving people. It engages them to focus on something other than themselves. Missions has effectively changed the hearts of scores of our young people through the years to activate them in giving and serving something that is bigger than themselves. Many of them continue to serve and support mission works and missionaries years after experiencing life on a short-term missions trip. I am grateful especially to Dan Slater for the years he has invested in young lives by taking them to mission fields to help with various projects. It is always a daunting task, but Dan has been relentless in making sure that young people are given the opportunity.

Dan has developed a favor among the missionaries who are members of our conference. He is very relational in his approach to everyone. He has a passion for missions and a love to serve. I have appointed him as my successor to oversee the mission work of the church. I will continue to work with him and with the missionaries as God leads me. My heart's desire and prayer continues to be for God to raise up a greater vision for missions ministries within the churches of our nation. A new generation is rising to the call of God to expedite the gospel to the nations. It is a generation that has the tools and ingenuity to get the work done. We must prepare ourselves as the church of the 21st century to provide the tools for the workers and let them do it! This statement is true: "The work which centuries might have done, now crowd the hours of setting sun" (Clara Thwaites, The Church Missionary Gleaner, 1890).

Chapter 19
Malawi

In 2005, at Elim Church in Houston, Texas I was introduced to a gentleman from the country of Malawi, Africa. He was in the U.S. to finish a degree at the University of Texas at San Antonio (UTSA). His name was James Nyondo. His father was a paramount chief of the Lambia tribe, which extends into the countries of Malawi, Zambia and Tanzania.

James had listened to the message that I had spoken in the morning session of the conference. He heard me tell about my worldview of Christianity and its message of the gospel to be preached in every nation of the world. He left the meeting telling me that he was going to contact me.

A few days later he called me and wanted to meet with me. He flew to Minneapolis, and we brought him to Shell Lake for a few days. James was a believer and follower of Christ. His plans were to become a leader of his country and apply the principles of Jesus' teachings from the Gospels.

We introduced James to our congregation, and they all were honored to meet him. I set up an interview for James with some people whom I felt would benefit from his story. The people who gathered were John and Colleen Smith from Superior, Wisconsin. Paul Tucker was also with us as well as Steve Salowitz who had been a missionary living in Tanzania for fourteen years. Steve works with the Seed Company which is a subsidiary of Wycliffe Bible Translators.

Our meeting with James opened the door to connect with the people of Malawi. The nation of Malawi is among the poorest nations in the world. James wanted to change that condition and set his goals to someday become the president of the country of Malawi.

James returned to Malawi after graduating from UTSA. He also held a law degree from the University of Johannesburg, South Africa. I wasn't sure why God chose James and me to become close friends. James called me a spiritual father and seemed to trust me. I was twenty-five years older than James.

In 2006 Paul Avery, David Lusse and I traveled to Malawi and were met by James at the airport in Lilongwe, the capital city of Malawi.

James took us to a retreat compound where we met his mother and father. I had brought a nice Bible to present to this highly regarded chief. We spent the afternoon together discussing the many needs of the Malawian people. I expressed the desire to build a center for worship and other uses in the community. James' mother was battling asthma and was open to permit us to pray over her for healing. God was gracious to give her immediate relief and opened up her breathing. She was very happy and made an offer to provide a piece of land where we could build a center for worship whenever the time was right.

James took us outside of the city to an area of land that he wanted to see developed for a school and a church. He also wanted a place to provide medical assistance for women to have a safe and sterile place for their babies to be born. He wanted to have fresh water for the people to drink. All I could see was a dry, desolate landscape that seemed impossible to develop. But God saw something different.

I was very surprised as we drove down an old dusty trail and came to a large canvas canopy with about a hundred men standing under it. I was told that these men were a group of chiefs who represented dozens of villages in the region. They would be like Mayors of our communities in Wisconsin. There were several hundred men all dressed in colored uniforms and turban caps standing on the outside of the canopy. I was told that these were officials in the communities from the region. At the center of the canopy sitting in the front was the head chief over that region. He was one of four of the most important chiefs who were leaders of the country. James told me that he was a very important man. I presented this chief with a very nice Bible with the compliments of Shell Lake Full Gospel Church in Shell Lake, Wisconsin.

My next assignment was to speak for twenty minutes to these chiefs and to another eight thousand people who had gathered at the site to observe all the ceremonies at this event.

I honestly didn't know what all was taking place except we knew that James was held in high esteem by these people who had heard that he was going to be there.

There were various groups of people from area villages who were performing skits and dances in front of James and the head chief. If they were impressed by the performing groups, they would walk up to the performers and place some money on the ground. It was evident that there were some performances that did not impress James and the chief.

James spoke to the people for about a half hour. I didn't know what he was telling them but saw him point to his Bible several times. When James was done speaking, he introduced me to come and speak to the people. I had only the use of a large battery-operated megaphone. We did not have any electricity. There were several thousand people looking at me to hear what I would say.

There was no recording of what I said. But I do remember that I talked to them about a God of plenty. A God who cares about all of their needs. A God who had a better future planned for them. I told them that if they would believe and trust God's only son to be their Savior and Lord, that their lives could be changed and that God could change their circumstances and provide better schooling, better health conditions, and better water sources. I didn't realize until a few years later that some of those words had been prophetic.

It was Jeff Rogers who I had introduced to James that God used to bring those words to pass. Jeff had been evicted from Zimbabwe, but his heart was to help the poor in Africa. His contact with James opened the door for Jeff to develop a large complex outside of Lilongwe which includes a medical clinic, nursing school, and education center. It is self-sustaining through energy provided by solar powered panels. Wells have been dug to provide fresh water throughout the area. The entire complex has become a prototype to the government of Malawi who is looking at it as a sustainable energy source for other parts of the country.

So, if you are wondering where Jeff Rogers built this magnificent complex for the glory of God, it sits on the site where I had spoken several years earlier when I stated that God had a better future planned for the people of Malawi. At that time, I had no idea about any of Jeff Roger's plans for doing anything in Malawi.

John and Colleen Smith developed a close relationship with James after our initial meeting together in Shell Lake. Both of them had missionary hearts and traveled to Malawi to see what God had in mind for them there.

God gave the Smiths favor with the people in the city which gave Colleen opportunities to teach on "Leadership Principles" to some of the government chiefs. She taught Bible classes, and God used her and John to train potential spiritual leaders.

In 2009 they planted "New Beginnings" Church and started a preschool which has 240 children attending. Along with Colleen's father, Paul Tucker, they have ordained six pastors which has resulted in seven churches established in Malawi.

James failed in his election bid for president of Malawi. He returned to Johannesburg to receive further education. He and his wife resided there and because of constant surveillance from his government, he could not continue to make contact with me.

On one occasion, while they lived in San Antonio, there was an attempt made on his life. His would-be assassins were arrested in New York. We had many intimate conversations. James told me how some large Christian television ministries had exploited him for their purposes after failing to live up to their promises of support to help his country. He lost trust in some Christian ministries and quoted from Mahatma Gandhi, the Hindu nationalist leader, "I like your Christ, I do not like your Christians. Your Christians are so unlike your Christ."

James considered our relationship and his relationship with the church congregation in Shell Lake as a time to restore his faith in authentic Christianity. He believed that we were true Christians and wasn't apprehensive or inhibited around us. We showed him how to have some fun in life. He had never grown up with toys and never played with other boys. His life was sheltered and controlled. We even took him on a snowmobile ride. He drove one across the frozen lake not knowing that water was under him. When we told him about that, he couldn't believe it. He had never seen a frozen lake.

James was a regal looking man. He was tall, handsome, and always wore a wide, bright smile. He was soft spoken and highly intelligent.

I was sad to learn that in July 2015, James passed away due to a fast growing cancer while in Pretoria, South Africa. That is the same city where I had lifted the power switch to turn on the electricity for the Bible college that Ron Kinnear had started.

James was only 47 years old when he died. He left his wife and two young sons behind. It did not seem to me that his work was done. Our first meeting at Elim Church in Houston, Texas was appointed by God. He knew James had a heart to see his nation turn to Christ and without our connection which led to our meeting with John and Colleen Smith, those churches would not be established in Malawi. James' death was not in vain. A spiritual legacy continues through the pastors that have been trained and ordained by three of the people who sat in our meeting with James at Full Gospel Church. They are Paul Tucker and John and Colleen Smith. God may bury the workman, but He does not bury the work.

Chapter 20
Color of Evangelism

When I was twelve years old, it seemed that all of my friends who were the same age were also all about the same size. I didn't have any problem with that. My problem was during the next few years when most of my boyhood friends began shooting up in size, I seemed to grow more slowly and fell way behind.

In sports, I had to practice twice as hard and long to compete for equal positions as the other players. Whenever teams were formed to play against each other, I would cringe with fear that I would be the last one chosen to play on one of the teams. Rather than be the last one chosen, I set my goal to become a captain who could choose the members of my town team. A competitive spirit got a hold on me, and I never gave less than one hundred percent effort of anything I did, except with academics.

I never liked to sit too long in one place without talking to somebody. I have always been a talker, and I've spent a good portion of my life learning from other people's experiences. The call to ministry has changed my attitude toward concentrated times of study, especially toward studying God's word.

God gave me a sanguine temperament which is supposed to indicate an outgoing type of personality. In high school that led me to audition for school musicals. I was selected to have the male leads in the musical, "Annie Get Your Gun", and "Oklahoma." I didn't realize at the time that performing before large audiences would help give me the confidence to stand before church audiences to preach God's word.

Participating in the school choir and chorus and learning to develop voice range and pitch from a skilled teacher helped prepare me for another future assignment. Harris Balko spent much time to help develop my voice which I used to perform in solo ensembles. It gave me the confidence to sing in front of people.

Four of us guys trained under Mr. Balko to develop a barbershop quartet. After high school graduation, our group entertained in area supper clubs where we passed the hat to receive a little spending money. We called ourselves "The Blue Boys." Our group auditioned for a television show known as The Ted Mack Amateur Hour. We came very close to winning. My decision to obey Christ's call for my life broke up our group the following year.

These musical opportunities prepared me for becoming worship leader in the church I pastored during the early years. I also have had many opportunities to sing solos in churches and conferences as well as weddings and funerals all through our ministry. I have always been comfortable in front of people which is a result of performing in my high school years. It seems that God was preparing me without my knowledge for what He had planned for my life.

I have always loved sports and adventure. The ministry afforded me the opportunities for both. One of the first things we did after settling into Shell Lake was to organize a church softball league. The area churches were ready for it. We welcomed both men and women to join their church teams. Many of the churches in Washburn County fielded a team, and we scheduled a game for each team one night every week. The enthusiasm from each team made it fun and competitive. We scheduled tournaments at the end of each season and gave out great trophies to the winning teams. Shell Lake Full Gospel got more than our share of trophies through the years. I continued to play slow pitch softball with the church until I reached fifty-four years of age.

Camp

In the early 1970's, Pastor Nelson Clair, myself, and our wives organized our first youth camps which we held at the Baptist Campground in Chetek, Wisconsin.

Nelson Clair was pastor of Lakeshore Tabernacle in Kenosha, Wisconsin, and his church would bring the children and youth all the way to Chetek. We had the shorter distance to travel from Shell Lake.

The Baptist Campground was rustic, with cabins that only had screens for windows. There were bathrooms and showers on each end of the campground with the girls on one and the boys on the other. The chapel was a rustic-style building with cement floor and wooden pews to sit on. It was located next to the lake. We had loud music and praise services in the evenings. People living around the lake could hear us worshiping fervently but never complained.

Our camp was heavily supported by volunteers from our churches who did the cooking and served as cabin and group counselors. We started out with about one hundred campers and continued to grow every year as we added more churches to our camp. Our sports program was second to none with activities that could involve every young camper. The altar services were full of young lives encountering God and the Holy Spirit. So many young lives have been saved at a youth camp. So many friendships have been developed that have continued even until now, two generations later.

Pastor Clair, myself, and our wives continued to direct the youth camps for nineteen years until turning it over to another couple, Steve and Tamara Waderich from Minneapolis. They moved the location of the camp twice, where now after over forty-five years, it is located in a luxurious campground on Spencer Lake near Waupaca, Wisconsin. Several more churches have joined the camp, and now there are over five hundred students who attend each year.

There are many stories to be told about camp exploits and experiences. Camp leaders deal with everything that happens.

During one camp at Chetek, my wife and I were awakened at 1:00 a.m. by the sound of some camp boys singing loudly. Their song was "O Christmas Tree." I ran over to the boy's cabin and found that they had wrapped toilet paper all around a tall pine tree that was in front of the cabin. The boys were laughing and quickly ran to their beds when I came. The tree was covered with paper.

Everything got quiet, so I went into the boy's bathroom and took away every roll of paper that was there. I hid them and walked into the boy's cabin and turned on the light. I told the boys that all the rolls of toilet paper were gone, and if they needed any paper, they would only get what was available on the tree. It was humorous to see how fast the paper disappeared from the pine tree.

It is rewarding to see how many of the churches who participate in youth camp have church leaders today who were once youth campers. I have met many married couples who first met their mate as a youth camper. Now they send their children to youth camp.

There are thousands of young lives who have experienced life, love, and Jesus at a youth camp since it first started in 1975.

Easter Alive

One of the best tools of evangelism for Full Gospel Church has been from the powerful production of our Easter Drama. This drama was performed five times each year for seventeen years. Every performance was followed by an invitation for salvation. There were many people who came to know Christ every year.

The Easter Alive drama was written and directed every year by Jennifer Slater. Her talent for casting and directing the musical portions of each show was absolutely amazing. Every year people came from a hundred-mile radius to see the play. The church gained a well-known reputation throughout the area communities for these exceptional performances.

Jennifer Slater has been my right hand in the ministry for many years. She and her husband Dan have a passion for the people to be mentored and matured in their walk of faith in the Lord.

They have produced more leaders and activated more volunteers in the church than anyone else. They are my spiritual children who have eased the load of the ministry for me, especially in my later years. They have prayed their four children through difficult times in their lives, and all of them are now serving the Lord. Dan has taught us that parents must never give up battling for your children's faith when the evil one tries to seduce them. God works with us when we work with Him.

Dan has taken many groups of men and youth from the church on outings into Canada and the lakes of the northern Minnesota boundary waters. His influence has helped maintain men's interest in the church. He has left many good impressions on young people's lives by his display of love and his passion for growing boys into men and girls into ladies. Dan has established his own spiritual legacy into the lives of hundreds of young men and women that have continued on to serve the Lord and raise their own families. I could never count all the Sunday nights Dan has gathered with the youth at the Uturn Center to minister and to mentor the youth in our community and the church.

The Uturn Center

Dan always has looked for ways to establish relationships between our church and the Shell Lake community. He loves to serve the people in our community. His favorite way of serving is to cook on the church grill which he and some guys in the church custom-made to serve large numbers of people. He has grilled meals for various organizations in the community as acts of appreciation for their services, including the entire staff of school teachers during their in-service day before the start of the school year.

Every year since the start of our first missions conference, we have set Tuesdays of the conference as a time for a lady's luncheon and a men's steak feed. The ladies meet at the church fellowship hall and the men meet in the country at the home of Bob and Marilyn Erwin.

Dan Slater puts his team together to prepare steaks on the grill to feed over 120 men. This includes the men missionaries attending the conference and guest pastors and leaders. Lasting friendships have been cultivated by time spent together, and new acquaintances are made every year. All of this takes place while the magnificent colors of the autumn leaves are falling to the ground as they leave the branches of the great oak and maple trees which stand in Bob Erwin's yard. It is a highlight event for the men who attend.

I'm grateful for Dan and Jen Slater who grew up in the church with a desire to serve the Lord and a heart to serve in ministry. Through the hurts and pain that comes with leadership in ministry, they have both kept a right spirit and have been faithful to serve and help carry out the vision God has given me. I honor them both for a job well done.

Chapter 21
Love the People

God permitted Linda and me to live out our lives in the same area where we were born. We were both born in Rice Lake and have never lived more than twenty-five miles from the city. We consider ourselves to be fortunate to have lived near some of our family, especially to remain near to both our parents until they passed away.

It never entered our thoughts or discussion that one day I would be able to travel across the world to meet people from cultures I knew nothing about.

God has filled my heart with a deep love for people. It doesn't seem to matter what color or nationality they are. I really do love all people. That doesn't mean that I have been loved by all people. I have endured more than a few unkind letters and phone calls from Christians who sounded like they preferred I do something other than stay on the pulpit. All pastors must learn how to live with criticism. The most important thing is to not hold offenses toward anyone or harbor any resentment. I have felt the hurt from rejection at times but cannot afford the luxury of entertaining unforgiveness in my heart. I have taken the position of Apostle Paul, "… I exercise myself to have always a conscience void of offense toward God, and toward men" (Acts 24:16 KJV).

When I first started out in ministry, I was told by my pastor to not expect that everyone will speak well of me. He said that experiencing rejection is part of the ministry. I remember a statement that he made to me when he said, "When you have been treated like a low-down, cur dog and still desire to preach, then you know you are called."

I think that my pastor must have had some hard experiences with some people. Actually, I think he brought some of that upon himself. He was quite an austere person.

There have been some who have challenged my position at times. One man stood in my office and called me an inappropriate name and wiped his feet off hard on the carpet and left. He never came back. Another man came into my office to tell me that he thought I had lost my mind and needed to see a shrink. I had to check with my elders to see if they felt the same way about me. Thank God they thought my mind was still okay.

I don't want to bring up any more incidents because it might sound like these things still resonate in my heart. They really don't because I have forgiven from my heart, and these people are gone anyway.

The point is, no one can survive fifty years of pastoring one congregation in a small community if they are not a loving and forgiving person. Everybody changes through time. Hopefully, those changes include becoming a more kind, caring, loving, patient, gentle, and forgiving person. Life is too short to spend it holding on to grudges, resentments, and unforgiveness. God never changes the way He thinks about you. Always remember. "The Lord is good, His unfailing love continues forever, and His faithfulness continues to each generation" (Psalm 100:5 NLT).

I have always tried to believe the best about people. Temperaments and personalities are different in everyone. Being a little naive has helped me to not judge others too quickly and maybe I have erred a little bit on the side of grace with them. I've been accused of having too much grace sometimes.

If we could better understand God's love and longsuffering toward us, we would be less opinionated and condemning of others. To love others is God's commandment, whether we find it easy or hard to do. It is not hard to love people when they agree with you. The test of love comes when you are afflicted by someone who is irritated in their spirit and decides to spread vicious slander against you. This has become more common with the negative and disrespectful attitudes the society has toward those who are in authority.

Those of us who have been given spiritual authority as leaders of faith must hold to certain boundaries in the scripture that remain timeless truths which we must not change. There is constant pressure to make compromises in order to make people feel good no matter if they are living right or not. It is difficult to not take it personal when people leave the church because we don't preach what they want to hear. It helped me to listen to a pastor friend speaking at a ministerial conference say, "God calls pastors to set the culture and DNA of our church. It's the culture of your church that dictates who comes and who stays. There are people who cannot go where you are going. People who defy the culture do not stay in the church. People who are extracted out of our church, and sometimes out of our lives, will be okay. God is still with them." I do believe that they will be okay.

There are always some people who resist change. I have discovered that even though change can be difficult, it usually makes things work better. That's why we have continued to change some of the methods of how we do things. We did not change our message. Our mission statement for the church is to "Know God, Grow People, Love the World." That involves developing a style or new method which still represents a church culture and can reach people for Jesus. New methods involve change, which can be hard for people to accept, but we must be willing to change if it can help us to reach people to God.

The challenge to be a pastor in the 21st Century is to be inclusive, drawing all age groups together in the church to love and serve each other without being forced to change the style that they enjoy. God has given me plenty of time to set the culture and DNA of Full Gospel Church. I have been charged to guard someone else's flock—God's flock. (see Acts 20:28)

I never owned the ministry God gave to me. I have always only been a steward of it. My heavenly father owns it. It seems that some people think that my ministry answers to them. I know that I have not done everything right with what God has entrusted to me. However, after fifty years of managing what God has entrusted to me, my conscience remains clear. My Lord himself will examine that, and He will decide the outcome of the ministry He has given me. My prayer is to hear Him say that I was a faithful servant. Paul wrote, "... it is required in stewards, that a man be found faithful" (1 Corinthians 4:2 KJV).

Jesus said, "... 'A faithful, sensible servant is one to whom the master can give the responsibility of managing his other household servants and feeding them. If the master returns and finds that the servant has done a good job, there will be a reward'" (Luke 12:42-43 NLT).

In the end, it will not be how much we have done in our lifetime, nor how much success others may see, that brings the Lord's commendation. It is to the stewards (managers) who are faithful to what He has called us to do that He will commend in the end. My life and ministry I leave in the hands of my faithful Lord who is the judge of all things.

When I was away from God during my late teens, I was tormented by a spirit of darkness. I had known God as a young boy and deeply loved Jesus. My belief in Jesus was not popular with my boyhood friends, and I was ridiculed for my childlike faith. I didn't want to be unpopular because of my Christian beliefs, so I compromised them.

That opened the door for evil spirits to entice me to turn away from God. I yielded to all the temptations that were available at that time. I lived a life of lies. In a short time, my conscience was defiled, and I turned to blaspheme God in hopes that He would forget about calling me to become a minister. I was no longer a loving person. I became a selfish person and wanted to do everything I was told I couldn't. I rebelled against God, against my family, and against the church. All this time I was lying to myself that I was happy and having fun.

During this journey into darkness, an evil spirit entered into me. It tormented me, and I often wrestled with a spirit of fear, especially during the night. I went from party time drinking to nonstop drinking in order to numb my fears from its torment.

My mother's prayers were also nonstop as she claimed me back to God and to the call upon my life that God had spoken to her while I was still in her womb.

When I tried to join the Air Force at eighteen years old, Mom drove me to the Federal Building in Minneapolis to go through the pre-induction physical. I thought that I would be leaving from there to take basic training at Lackland Air Force Base in San Antonio, Texas. I failed the physical because the eczema on my hands began to inflame just as I was being examined for any marks or scars on my body. I couldn't' believe how red my hands looked at that moment as I had never seen them like that.

As I left the room and walked out into the large hallway that looked over the bus station that would not be taking me to the airport, I saw a lone figure standing in the doorway at the end of the hallway. I knew that it was my mother. She had waited for me because she knew that God had called me to serve Him, not to join the service. I was angry and crying at the same time. I had just been rejected from serving in the military and was angry at my mother because I knew inside of me that she had something to do with it. I can remember how ashamed and lowly I felt as she drove me back home.

I was glad to have Linda in my life as my girlfriend because she kept reminding me how glad she was that I was still home. I battled the darkness in my life for another year before I finally surrendered to Jesus and was delivered from those evil spirits as God filled up my life with His Holy Spirit. I was radically changed then, and I'm still radically changed now. All of the darkness that was inside of me was filled with light, and I felt that I could never get enough of His presence in me. I was also baptized with a new love for Him and a new love for others.

People often will make mention that they notice how much love I have for people. I have just described to you my bad times and the dark times of my life. God has forgiven me much. That is why I love much. When I meet people whose lives have been beaten up by sin and guilt and shame, I am moved to love them to a forgiving and healing Jesus. If He can do it for me, He can do it for anybody. True love is freedom. There is no greater need in the world than to be loved. There is no greater love than to offer your life to help someone else. Jesus demonstrated His love for us when he died for us while we were still sinners.

In Luke's gospel, there was an immoral woman who offered her broken life to the mercy of Jesus. The religious wondered why Jesus would allow himself to be seen with her. Jesus told the religious the story of a man who loaned money to two people. To one he loaned a lot of money and to the other he loaned a small amount of money. Neither of the two men could repay the loan so they both were forgiven of their debt. Jesus asked the religious a question, "Who do you suppose loved him more after that?" The answer was, "The one for whom he canceled the larger debt." Then Jesus said, "I tell you, her sins—and they are many—have been forgiven, so she has shown me much love. But a person who is forgiven little shows only little love" (Luke 7:47 NLT).

This story explains why God has gifted me with much love. I feel forgiven of much sin. Love must be given away. It is a fruit of the Holy Spirit. It grows the more it is used. When we give our love to others, it will return to you in full—pressed down, shaken together to make room for more, running over, and poured into your lap. The best way to keep your love tank full is to keep giving it away. It is expressed best with a smile, a touch, a kind word, a note of appreciation, a thank you, a helping hand, a little extra time, a hug, or a word of encouragement.

As I leave the pastorate after fifty years, I will take with me the memories of the wonderful people who

156

shared their love with Linda and me in both big and small ways. The appreciation cards, the gifts, the meals together, the hugs, and all the encouraging words that have expressed your approval toward us. Who wouldn't want to pastor a congregation of people like that? We have laughed and cried together, and we have prayed through many crises together. We are a family who has learned much about each other and have loved one another with Christ-like love.

Our daughter Angel was the first person who I ever heard sing the Valedictory address at her high school graduation in 1988. The song she sang was, "Love In Any Language."

"Love never fails. And now abide faith, hope, love there; but the greatest of these is love" (1 Corinthians 13:8,13 NKJV).

Chapter 22
Relationships Are Reciprocal

For a church plant to survive more than 50 years, it must survive the shifts and changes and excesses that take place throughout the church world. There is always the temptation to try to copy the pattern of success that someone else might have. There are tendencies toward extremes that must be carefully examined for imbalances.

Our church eldership has worked hard to stay balanced with both our style and doctrine. We have kept evangelism the main thrust of the church vision. I think that every church has its own uniqueness, and every church could tell its own story.

I have written this story to bring encouragement and hope to the hearts of church leaders and congregation members who may not feel that what is happening in their church has much significance. God assures us that He is faithful to every promise that He has given to us. We just need to "... hold fast to the confession of our faith without wavering, for He who promised is faithful" (Hebrews 10:23 NKJV).

Full Gospel Church is motivated to obey the "Great Commission" of Christ. We have looked for ways to touch the nations and to bless them as well as assist the needs of missionaries through creative financial support.

Missions activates people to get involved with something bigger than themselves. I have seen many people in the church who got excited and interested in church life after they began to partner with our missions ministry.

One of my greatest joys of the ministry has been that of building relationships with so many pastors and leaders across the nation. I joined the International Ministerial Association in 1967 and a few years later started attending the national conferences. The conferences were generally held in the large churches once every year in various cities around the southern, central, and western states. Through my association with the I.M.A., I made friends with many ministers. Over the year those friendships grew, and I began to exchange pulpit ministry with several of them. This cultivated growth in my capacity to speak outside of my own pulpit.

I remember taking my family to Chico, California in 1980 to speak at the Paradise Youth Camp. That opportunity gave my wife and children the chance to see the majestic giant Sequoia Redwoods. We traveled to the Black Hills to see Mt. Rushmore and came home through the Badlands in South Dakota. It was a great outing for my family.

Linda and I enjoy our times when we attend the I.M.A. general board planning sessions every April. For many years we would meet in Estes Park, Colorado. Glen

Zeazle lived in Denver and would host our group by guiding brief tours of that area. He was a special minister friend.

I still serve on the I.M.A. general board and for the past several years we held our planning sessions in Branson, Missouri. We always take some time aside to visit some of the shows there. It is a fun place to relax. We love the beautiful lakes and hills that surround Branson.

I've had the joy of taking many minister friends on fishing trips into Canada. These are fly-in trips to outpost cabins that are owned by Shad and Jamie Torgerson whose family have been friends with us since they were young boys. They own the Dogskin Lake Lodge and Outposts cabins that sit each on separate lakes.

The lakes we fish are full of walleye and northern pike. Most of my minister friends who come from Texas and Louisiana will fly to Winnipeg. I pick them up at the airport and drive to the Winnipeg River where a float plane takes us to the cabin. We spend four or five nights before returning home. Everybody catches fish, and the fellowship at our table of fried walleye is unsurpassed.

There is a small trade-off to these trips where I have helped guide my hunting and fishing minister friends.

Bill Butler invited me to hunt deer and wild pigs in Alabama.

Richard Beatty took me fishing off the coast of Louisiana.

Ron Nissen fishing off the Houston Gulf.

James Hartley put me on the large crappies in East Texas.

John Mortimer took us fishing for Peacock bass on the Amazon River.

This all resulted from the great relationships that have developed through reaching beyond ourselves to make lifetime friends.

The congregation of Full Gospel Church has done much more than financially support missionaries. Many of them stay connected through regular communication with those whom they have befriended. It is real life to life relationship. There is a spirit of joy and love that is attached to those relationships. Our missionaries consider Shell Lake a second home and a place where they can relax and be themselves, and they tell me how much they look forward to the time when they can attend our missions conference.

Most of the people from our church who have visited a mission work on a short-term basis have had their lives changed forever.

One such man was Bob Jetto. Bob and his wife Debbie came to know the Lord through Jeff and Sue Burch. The Burch's had a dramatic change in their lives after encountering God's forgiveness and salvation early on in their marriage. Jeff worked in construction, and Bob Jetto was working with him. Bob Jetto saw the change in Jeff's life, and it moved him to make his own commitment to follow the Lord. The Burch's and Jetto's became active members of our church.

Jeff trained Bob as a carpenter and eventually Bob formed his own construction company. When the church added on a large addition to its complex in 1995, Bob Jetto was hired to be the contractor.

The church had plans set to build the new addition in 1985 as we had a growth spurt at that time and the sanctuary had filled up. But God had a different timing in His mind. For one thing, we did not have funds to build, and we probably would have had to secure a loan from the bank.

Also, at the same time, we were drawing up plans for an addition, we were met with some unusual circumstances. Another ministry had moved into the area that featured some supernatural giftings. There were many people from the area who were drawn to support it. When a new church started near Spooner, it drew people from other churches in the communities to give their support. Several people left our church. This changed our plans for needing an addition to our facility.

It was ten years later before we began the building project which was completed in 1995 at a cost of $350,000.00. This time, it was God's clear plan, and it was done the way God wanted us to do it—debt-free!

The story behind this is that the church, which was started near Spooner, had a serious failure and was closed down after five years. We were blessed to receive a number of our former members back into our fellowship.

The elders had the faith to believe that God would supply the means for us to build the addition if we would commit to it. I will admit that my faith was weak to believe that we could build that large an addition debt-free. God tested me through that whole process, and there were times where my faith wavered. But the elders were confident, and I trusted their faith. We saw the process gain slowly at times but also continually. Whenever the money was gone as we were building, more amounts would come in to keep going. That's the way it continued until the project was completed. God always came through, even if it was at zero hour. Honestly, we never had to hold the project up very long before more funds would come in to keep going. At the end when the building project was finished, it was all paid for.

Bob Jetto gave us some breaks with his labor, and we were appreciative for all of his support to the end.

On two occasions, Bob Jetto joined up with mission trips into Mexico and Peru. I was with him when he went to Zacatecas, Mexico. Our missionary friends, Richard and Sally Amezquita, introduced us to a new church there and Bob and I ministered in the church.

Bob was always a joy to be around. He loved life, and he loved people. He was drawn to people in poverty and need. He prayed for people in Mexico with much compassion. He told me that he felt God's call to be a missionary. He and Debbie both felt that calling.

Bob's second trip was to Iquitos, Peru to help the Mortimers build a church building. The Mortimers have told me how dedicated Bob was working long hours in the torrid heat to get as much accomplished as he could. Everyone knew how much Bob loved missions work.

Bob also had a passion for the outdoors. He loved to hunt and fish. He really loved to hunt ducks. I remember us heading out to hunt ducks on Lincoln Lake early before daybreak. We loaded his ten-foot flat bottom Jon boat with several bags of decoys, his retriever dog, two guns, several boxes of ammunition, and the two of us. Bob weighed about a hundred pounds more than me. I couldn't see anything in the dark as he rowed to our blind. I did feel the water which was only about two inches below the gunnels of his boat. My hands held tightly to its sides while wondering if there was a chance that we could sink our overloaded little boat. I asked Bob if he was sure we would make it to his blind. He told me that if we didn't make it, we would only sink in less than three feet of water. He knew where we were all the time.

Bob was a star softball player on our church team. He batted left-handed and helped us win a lot of games over the years with his long home runs. He was competitive, yet had an easy-going nature. Everybody loved him.

In February of 2004, Bob and Debbie had their plans set to go on a vacation cruise to the Caribbean. Kevin and Diane Livingston would join them on their cruise.

The day before they were to leave, Bob was working on building a house for his father near Bob's home. He stepped on an unbraced piece of flooring and fell into the basement, landing on his head. The damage swelled his brain to where it was unstoppable, and Bob passed away on March 6th in Duluth, Minnesota. He was 45 years old.

The service for Bob was the largest attended funeral in my 50 years of pastoring the church. The church received many calls of tributes to Bob Jetto from his many missionary friends around the world.

Bob is gone from us to be with the Lord, but he will not be forgotten in the hearts of all the people who knew him and loved him. His wife Debbie has courageously continued on with her life and her ministry. She is currently working to help bring healing and support to women in crises. Her goal is to have a center for women that provides a place of recovery for them.

Chapter 23
A Generational God

God's salvation in the Amundson family began with my grandmother, my dad's mother. When my father was saved, he became the second generation. I became the third generation and our three children the fourth generation to serve Christ. Our grandchildren now are serving Christ and are fifth generation believers. We have great-grandchildren who are growing up in a Christian home and will be the sixth generation who will be taught to receive God's salvation.

God holds every parent responsible for telling His Word to their children. "Telling to the generations to come the praises of the Lord, and His strength and His wonderful works that He has done. — That the generation to come might know them, the children who would be born, that they may arise and declare them to their children, — That they may set their hope in God" (Psalm 78:4,6,7a NKJV).

The call to be God's steward is the call to be a faithful manager of all that God gives us to do. I have never taken this assignment from the Lord lightly. I hold a reverent fear and respect for my master since I have answered His call.

People occasionally will make a comment or attempt to encourage me by telling me that I have done my job well. Even though I appreciate hearing that, I know that the most important words for me to hear one day, are the words of my master who placed me as a steward over His work.

When my journey in this life is over and my work here is done, my hope and prayer is that my master and Lord will say, "Well done, good and faithful servant, you have been faithful over a few things, I will make you ruler over many things, enter into the joy of the Lord" (Matthew 25:21 NKJV).

In the end, it is not how successful we might appear in the eyes of others, but it will be whether we have been faithful to what God has called us to do that meets with His commendation.

I once read a comment by Frank Damazio, a great Bible teacher in Portland, Oregon. He said, "You can teach what you know, but you produce in others what you are."

A leader's life is on display for everyone to observe. Longevity is the test of character. If there are any ulterior motives to what you are doing, it will be revealed over time. Jesus explained how to detect wolves in sheep's clothing. "... you will know them by their fruits" (Matthew 7:20 NASB).

A minister friend once asked me if I could describe in one word what I thought would encapsulate the success of such a long time in ministry. I told him I believe that one word is, authenticity. I have tried to be as transparent with my life as possible. What you see in me is what you get. There is a vulnerability in that, and I have made it easy for some people to take potshots at my imperfections. I did mention that I'm not perfect, didn't I?

No one can escape the scrutiny of others when you are in the limelight. You just have to be comfortable in your own skin. Have I been hurt by people? Yes. Do I cry real tears? Yes. Do I get angry over injustices? Yes. Do my wife and I ever get into an argument? Yes. Have I ever suffered discouragement? Yes.

The saving grace for me with all of these emotions is that I have never languished very long with any of them. The antidote for stress, worry, or anxiety for me has been three things throughout my life.

- Number one: "Don't let the sun go down while you are still angry." (Ephesians 4:26b NLT).
- Number two: "In everything give thanks" (1 Thess 5:18a NKJV).
- Number three: "Rejoice in the Lord always" (Philippians 4:4 a KJV).

I once heard a pastor state that, "Pastoral leaders must guard their emotional well-being. It is not so much our I.Q. (intelligence quotient) that matters as it is our E.Q. (emotional quotient)." We must have enough well-being to properly handle rejection or disappointment.

My own well-being has come from the support, love, and encouragement of so many people I have been blessed to serve through the years. Every kind word, every note, card, and gift I have received has helped keep me confident and secure with my position as a pastor. Most people don't realize how much it means to receive their assurance and support.

My wife has always been my greatest confidence boost. The assurance that I receive from her love and support has been a constant reinforcement to never entertain the thought of quitting. Her faithfulness to me has always been a model of what true faithfulness really means.

Neither of us could have imagined in the beginning what God foresaw in His plans to increase us in our latter days. Our beginnings were so small. But we did apply ourselves to be faithful in the small things that He assigned to us. We were never capable at the beginning to "rule over many things" anyway. God has to trust us to be faithful in the least things before He can trust us to be faithful with much things. I first had to learn to preach to a small crowd before I was skilled enough to preach to large crowds.

It is like a dream for me to believe that God would permit me to travel to four continents across the globe from little Shell Lake, Wisconsin. A dream come true to preach the gospel and help to meet missionary's needs in so many nations through our church congregation.

Full Gospel Church is a congregation that is united around the common purpose of helping and blessing people. There is a continued flow of funds available when we invest in helping others. I have been privileged to pastor a congregation of generous people. Our church motto is: Living by giving, and loving by serving."

Proverbs 11:25 (NKJV) says. "The generous soul will be made rich, and he who waters others will also be watered himself." The NLT translation reads, "Those who refresh others, will themselves be refreshed." it's the law of sowing and reaping affect.

Time and again, within our church when someone has a crisis, there are those who step up to offer what assistance they can provide to help meet that need. God always seems to increase those people who have a generous heart to give. The scripture expresses it this way, "Yes, you will be enriched in every way so you can always be generous. And when we take your gift to those who need them, they will thank God" (2 Corinthians 9:11 NLT).

I have seen how real love responds to human need. I have learned that our efforts to help when a need arises is not about a few people doing everything—but love is about a lot of people doing something. That's how needs are met. That has become the M.O. of the church I have pastored for fifty years. It is the reason for our existence as a church.

I didn't know anything about planting a church when I first started in ministry. I just looked for a need, and with God's help, tried to fill it. When you fill someone's need, there is a change that takes place. They will listen to you, and that creates an opportunity to tell them about Jesus love.

Honor

Full Gospel Church honors people. We honor leaders in our community, and we honor our teachers and educators. We honor our veterans and our law enforcement officers. We honor our government officials and our medical staff who serve our needs. We look for ways to express gratefulness toward all of those groups who give themselves to serve us.

In our community the church has found ways to express appreciation to the various groups who serve our community.

Through the years we have sponsored dinners of appreciation by inviting the law enforcement people to come and be blessed by our church family. The same has been done for the veterans and for the medical people.

Dan Slater and his team use large grills to provide a cookout meal for all of the Shell Lake educators, custodians, and school bus drivers during the in-service day for the teachers at the beginning of the school year. It is our way to thank these people for all they do for the children in our community. We honor those to whom honor is due.

Blessing People

Full Gospel Church is united around the common purpose of blessing people.

One year Dan Slater went to the inner city of Minneapolis with a friend who worked with kids that were raised in the projects. They concocted a plan to take a bus load of those kids away from the concrete jungle and take them camping at a remote lake and woods in northern Wisconsin. The campsite was Leisure Lake, about twenty-five miles north of Shell Lake.

These kids were undisciplined and street-wise, and the goal was to isolate them long enough to get their attention and teach them about Jesus. It was also to give kids who had never been out of the city the experience of the country and wilderness life.

The first night around the campfire those kids sat in total awe at the bright starry sky. They had never seen the sky full of stars because of the bright lights of the city that blocked out their view.

I drove to the camp the next day to check on how Dan was doing with the kids. He and his team had laid out rules to try and keep order in the camp. One of the rules was that no one could walk off the grounds, or there would be consequences. To most of those kids, consequences meant nothing. A group of them rebelled on the second day and decided they would walk off the campground and find their way back to Minneapolis. I drove around the corner and met them first just as they were leaving. I asked Dan what I should do with them, and he told me to just let them go.

The group was told by Dan that as soon as they got out of his sight, they could not come back to the camp. He told them that the first inhabited property was about three miles away and that the woods was full of bears and wolves. They would be on their own after they left his sight.

I stood with Dan watching that group of boys slowly shuffle their feet as they walked almost out of sight. They looked back at us and then slowly turned around and shuffled their feet back to camp. There were relatively few problems after that.

There is a couple in the church whose ministry is to serve food to those in our county who need it. Chuck and Sue Adams have devoted their retirement years establishing a county food pantry that serves hundreds of people every month. Chuck has given himself to assist those who are disabled with projects that need repair or with needs they are unable to meet. He established a monthly food distribution that started at Full Gospel Church and continued for several years. Chuck and Sue have united many volunteers around the common purpose of helping and blessing people.

Through the years, the church has sent teams of workers to help people recover from natural disasters such as the one from Hurricane Katrina that hit Mississippi and Louisiana in 2005. We rebuilt a house for a family whose home was flooded with four feet of water. In one week, we finished that house. Before we left, a Christmas tree was put up in their living room. It was the only piece of furnishing in the house. We placed gifts for each member of the family under the tree and held hands together as our group sang to them, "We wish you a Merry Christmas." It was Christmas for them even though the real Christmas was three months away. It was a heart-warming scene as tears ran down all of our faces.

As I write this story, another group of fourteen people from the church are in Denham Springs, Louisiana assisting that community with recovery from the worst flood in the history of that area. This group of people has rallied with the common purpose to help and bless the people in Louisiana.

Conclusion

I have been blessed to serve as pastor of Shell Lake Full Gospel Church for the past 50 years. I'm also a blessed father, grandfather, and great-grandfather who never dreamed of leaving a legacy of faith and faithfulness in a small town church that is touching the world for Christ. These things are very humbling, and I owe all the glory to God for all that He has done through us.

It is difficult to comprehend the fact that I have stayed long enough to have ministered to five generations. It started with a lady by the name of Katie Ladd who attended the church in the mid-1960's. She brought her granddaughter to the church in Shell Lake. Her name was Sandy. Sandy married Dr. Timothy Warner who is the pastor in Hayward, Wisconsin. One of their four children is the Children's Minister in Shell Lake. Her name is Katie Schrankel. Her grandparents are Jim and Rita Ladd who now attend the church in Shell Lake. Katie Schrankel, and her husband Chad have five children who are part of the church, which makes five generations from the Ladd family. How cool is that?

God is a generational God, and He loves it when families pass on their legacy of faith to their children and their children's children.

If you are a first generation believer, you have the wonderful opportunity to tell of God's wonderful works to the next generation so "That they may set their hope on God, and not forget the works of God, but keep His commandments" (Psalm 78:7 NKJV).

I could not have been called to a greater honor than that of being called to a pastor. To me, it represents a serious charge from God to be a guardian of His own flock. The church of God is extremely significant because "He purchased [it] with His own blood" (Acts 20:28 NKJV). Interestingly, the meaning of my name is "guardian of the flock."

God calls pastors to set the culture and DNA of the church that they oversee. The culture and style of Full Gospel Church are setup to reach people for Jesus. Not everyone who has come into the church has been able to assimilate into our style and culture. Whenever people have left the church, it was always difficult to accept, and I had to learn to not take it personally. There were people who could not go where we were going. I know that those who were extracted from us will be okay. God is with them. We can all still be happy because "joyful indeed are those whose God is the Lord" (Psalm 144:15b NLT).

The joy of seeing people's lives changed and the blessings that have followed our ministry has made every year worth serving the Lord.

The next generation of those that we have mentored and invested our lives in will take the mantle of faith and write their own stories. My successor, Reg Myers, and assistants Dan and Jen Slater, and my granddaughter's husband, Josiah Hodgett, are set to fulfill their own destiny of a life and ministry of faithful service to the Lord. And they will all be successful.

I'm not sure what the next season will be in my life, but I am sure that I am ready to embrace whatever season it is. I just want to be faithful in the season that God has for me. I do believe that God has a greater purpose for our lives. As Ephesians 5:16 NLT says, "Make the most of every opportunity ..." That, I intend to do.

God himself will examine all that we have done, and in the end, He will decide our judgment.

"Now, a person who is put in charge as a manager must be faithful. As for me, it matters very little how I might be evaluated by you or by any human authority. I don't even trust my own judgment on this point. My conscience is clear, but that doesn't prove I'm right. It is the Lord himself who will examine me and decide. So don't make judgments about anyone ahead of time—before the Lord returns. For He will bring our darkest secrets to light and will reveal our private motives. Then God will give to each one whatever praise is due" (1 Corinthians 4:2-5 NLT).

I will always be grateful for the support of all my minister acquaintances around the world, and for all the pastors who have ministered in our pulpit and who have shared their pulpits with me. I am grateful for the life work of all our missionary friends who sacrifice so many things of life to faithfully serve the call. I am grateful for every member of Full Gospel Church who has faithfully served the vision of your pastor over the past 50 years. I am willing to lay down my life for all of you.

I have embraced each of the seasons of my life without regret. God has been with me. The joy of the Lord has been my strength through each season.

As the season of pastoring in a small town church has ended, I look ahead to the new season God has for my wife and I. The experiences gained through each season has prepared me to give what I have learned unto others.

I once heard someone say that, "experiences may not be the best teacher, but to learn from other's experiences may be the best teacher." I have spent my life listening and learning from other's experiences, which helped me to avoid some things that they have learned the hard way. Many hard lessons can be avoided by listening to others.

My prayer is that we can still be a blessing to those still in the trenches who might need a battle-worn soldier to come alongside them for encouragement so they too can remain faithful to the end.

We have turned our ministry over to our team of successors who have faithfully served our ministry for many years. The team is under the leadership of Pastor Regan and Dawn Myers. They assume all properties of the church debt-free. God will bless and anoint all of their ministries as they journey forward.

I am grateful that you chose to read some of my life story and God's faithfulness to me. I am grateful that God has given me His story to write. To Him be all the glory for the great things He has done!

Pastor Virgil Amundson
virgilamundson2@gmail.com